Creative Projects
Big and Small

By the Editors of Time-Life Books

Alexandria, Virginia

Time-Life Books Inc.
is a wholly owned subsidiary of

Time Incorporated

FOUNDER: Henry R. Luce 1898-1967

Editor-in-Chief: Jason McManus

Chairman and Chief Executive Officer:
J. Richard Munro
President and Chief Operating Officer:
N. J. Nicholas, Jr.
Editorial Director: Ray Cave
Executive Vice President, Books: Kelso F. Sutton
Vice President, Books: George Artandi

Time-Life Books Inc.

EDITOR: George Constable
Executive Editor: Ellen Phillips
Director of Design: Louis Klein
Director of Editorial Resources: Phyllis K. Wise
Editorial Board: Russell B. Adams, Jr., Dale M.
Brown, Roberta Conlan, Thomas H. Flaherty, Lee
Hassig, Donia Ann Steele, Rosalind Stubenberg,
Henry Woodhead
Director of Photography and Research:
John Conrad Weiser
Assistant Director of Editorial Resources:
Elise Ritter Gibson

PRESIDENT: Christopher T. Linen
Chief Operating Officer: John M. Fahey, Jr.
Senior Vice Presidents: Robert M. DeSena, James L.
Mercer, Paul R. Stewart
Vice Presidents: Stephen L. Bair, Ralph J. Cuomo,
Neal Goff, Stephen L. Goldstein, Juanita T. James,
Hallett Johnson III, Carol Kaplan, Susan J.
Maruyama, Robert H. Smith, Joseph J. Ward
Director of Production Services:
Robert J. Passantino

Library of Congress Cataloging-in-Publication Data
Creative projects / by the editors of Time-Life
Books.
   p. cm.—(Successful parenting)
   Bibliography: p.
   Includes index.
   ISBN 0-8094-5937-X.
   1. Handicraft.   I. Time-Life Books.
   II. Series.
TT157.C725 1988   649'.51—dc19
                         87-33557
                               CIP
ISBN 0-8094-5938-8 (lib. bdg.)

Successful Parenting

SERIES DIRECTOR: Dale M. Brown
Series Administrators: Jane Edwin, Norma E. Shaw
Editorial Staff for *Creative Projects:*
Associate Editor/Research: Rita Thievon Mullin
Designers: Elissa Baldwin, Edward Frank
Picture Editor: Jane Jordan
Text Editors: Margery A. duMond, John Newton,
Moira J. Saucer
Researchers: Charlotte Fullerton, Sydney Johnson
Assistant Designer: Cynthia S. Capozzolo
Copy Coordinator: Ruth Baja Williams
Picture Coordinator: Linda Yates
Editorial Assistant: Jayne A. L. Dover

Special Contributors: Linda Blaser, Carol Boyd,
Alice Cannon, Nancy Cook, Vial Crouch, Mary
Hanrahan, Beecie Kupersmith, Holly Langenfeld,
Ann Miller, Margie Moore, Nancy Payne, Toni
Powell, Michael Shall, Lorene Steinberg, Dorothy
Wallace (projects), Betsy Frankel (text), Barbara
Cohn, Anne Muñoz-Furlong (research)

Editorial Operations
Copy Chief: Diane Ullius
Production: Celia Beattie
Library: Louise D. Forstall

Correspondents: Elisabeth Kraemer-Singh (Bonn);
Maria Vincenza Aloisi (Paris); Ann Natanson
(Rome).

First printing. Printed in U.S.A.

Published simultaneously in Canada.
School and library distribution by
Silver Burdett Company, Morristown, New Jersey
07960.

TIME-LIFE is a trademark of Time Incorporated
U.S.A.

Other Publications:

THE TIME-LIFE GARDENER'S GUIDE
MYSTERIES OF THE UNKNOWN
TIME FRAME
FIX IT YOURSELF
FITNESS, HEALTH & NUTRITION
HEALTHY HOME COOKING
UNDERSTANDING COMPUTERS
LIBRARY OF NATIONS
THE ENCHANTED WORLD
THE KODAK LIBRARY OF CREATIVE
   PHOTOGRAPHY
GREAT MEALS IN MINUTES
THE CIVIL WAR
PLANET EARTH
COLLECTOR'S LIBRARY OF THE CIVIL WAR
THE EPIC OF FLIGHT
THE GOOD COOK
WORLD WAR II
HOME REPAIR AND IMPROVEMENT
THE OLD WEST

*For information on and a full description of any
of the Time-Life Books series listed above, please
call 1-800-621-7026 or write:*
Reader Information
Time-Life Customer Service
P.O. Box C-32068
Richmond, Virginia 23261-2068

This volume is one of a series about raising
children.

The Consultant

Dr. Judith A. Schickedanz, a child development
expert, is an associate professor in the department
of Early Childhood Education and head of the
Early Childhood Learning Laboratory, an innova-
tive program for preschool children, both at the
Boston University School of Education. Her published titles include *Toward Understanding Children* and *Strategies for Teaching Young Children.*
She has also generated many scholarly articles and
presentations on concept development in children
and the role of play in early childhood learning
processes. She has been a consultant to the Children's Television Workshop, producers of *Sesame
Street,* as well as an active member of the National
Association for the Education of Young Children
and other professional organizations. Dr. Schickedanz is coordinator of the Early Childhood
Teacher Education Program at Boston University.

Contents

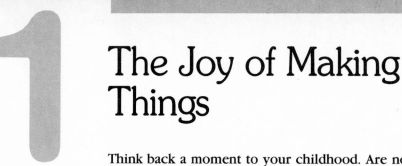

The Joy of Making Things

Think back a moment to your childhood. Are not some of your fondest recollections of those times when you made something—for yourself or for your mother, or even when in an inventive frame of mind you used your own face as a canvas and transformed it as the girl at right is doing? Many adults preserve such happy memories of childhood projects and of the joyous feelings that accompanied them. Something about those experiences made them so indelible. Perhaps it is the sense of adventure and creativity, the excitement of making something new, something by one's own hand, that sets such moments apart.

Your child is a wellspring of enthusiasm and ideas. She will gladly take on the role of creator, with just a little encouragement from you. And nothing could be more important to her development than to participate in a variety of arts and crafts activities. As this chapter suggests, she will have a great deal to gain from them, not least of which will be the wonderful memories they instill. If your own imagination fails you, trust hers. To inspire it, this book offers 104 projects to get her creative juices flowing.

All Children Are Creative

Children possess a natural and wonderful capacity to create. When your child squeezes a handful of clay into an irregular shape and declares excitedly, "Dog!" he is expressing his own unique vision. Whatever creative activity happens to be engaging his interest at the moment—whether it is sculpting a dog, making swirling patterns with finger paint, or sprinkling colored sand on a piece of construction paper that has been drizzled with wet glue—you can be sure that he has embarked upon a voyage of discovery. He will be learning not only about the qualities and properties of the materials that he uses, but also about his own ability to affect and change them. At the same time he will be gaining a sense of his specialness as a human being. And all the while he will be enhancing his imagination, improving his powers of perception, and honing his physical skills. Perhaps best of all, he will be having fun.

Elements of creativity
Creativity is the process of bringing something into being that was not there before. It involves putting together known elements and past experiences to produce newness. Even when a child does something as simple as mixing red and white paint and finds out for the first time that the two colors yield pink, he is being creative. To him, at least, his discovery is as fresh as the color pink itself.

Most children love making things and will throw themselves wholeheartedly into arts and crafts projects. As they paint a picture, glue bits of paper onto a collage, or mold a lump of clay into a pot, they are doing much more than just amusing themselves. Without their really being aware of it, they are developing in myriad ways.

A link to self-esteem
The act of creating something tangible gives a boost to your child's self-esteem—to his sense of the value of his own ideas and perceptions. Through art, he can organize his response to his world and have results to show for it as well. Along the way, he will have the opportunity to make decisions, meet challenges, and solve problems on his own. Which colors should he use? What kind of materials? Should he paint with a wide brush or a narrow one? By making choices like these, he builds self-assurance and independence. The work itself helps him define his identity. And when he is finished, his "See what I made!" is a statement of pride in his achievement.

An outlet for emotion
Besides building self-esteem, creative activities allow your youngster to express her inmost self. The sky is the limit, or so

it can seem. With coloring books, where boundaries exist and her crayon is not supposed to stray outside the lines, she cannot soar. But by actively exploring and creating with paints, crayons, paper, and glue—or with any other material that comes to hand—she can release emotion while giving free play to her imagination. Just watching the way your youngster applies paint to the paper can reveal much about how she is feeling. Does she slap it on with vehement, broad strokes? Perhaps she is letting out feelings of tension and frustration. Or does she brush the paper with a featherlight touch? She may be re-creating a happy moment. The colors that she chooses can tell a whole different story, expressing a full rainbow of moods and responses.

Painting or drawing can offer a very young child a way to express some of her thoughts and emotions, which she may not be old enough to communicate in words. She may use the activity as a way of letting out feelings of joy, sorrow, or pain. Then again, she may merely be experimenting or perhaps just passing the time; art may be an interlude between other activities or a respite from them. Children's art is not always a vehicle for emotional expression.

As a toddler works at painting or drawing a picture or at modeling a piece of clay, she is responding moment by moment to the experience. It is the process, more than the product itself, that is important to her. You may not be able to grasp precisely what your child has in her mind; her forms have definite meaning for her, but those meanings may well elude you. She herself may not be able to articulate her thoughts and feelings of the moment—but then why should she? In being creative, she is learning to feel good about herself, and with your encouragement she will want to go on and do more.

Working with the most basic material of all, mud, a boy does what generations of children have done before him and creates something to tickle his fancy—in this case, a birthday cake. The fertile imaginations of the young allow them to turn the ordinary into the extraordinary.

A total involvement

Your child's senses come into play when he is engaged in a creative activity. With his eyes, he takes in color, texture, and line. He smells the clay. He hears the crackle of newsprint as it is being torn from a long roll, and he feels the delicate texture of tissue paper betweeen his fingers. And if he is very young, he may even be likely to taste his art supplies—a good reason to make sure they are nontoxic.

The process of touching and handling things promotes your little artist's understanding of them. By manipulating the different materials that are used in arts and crafts activities, he comes to realizations about size, spatial relationships, and physical properties. Making a fabric collage, he learns to differentiate scraps of rough corduroy from snippets of smooth velvet. Working with wet clay, he learns the meaning of "soft." After the clay figure dries, he feels it and discovers "hard." All this direct experience sharpens his perception.

A boost to cognitive development

Creative activities have yet another major benefit. They stimulate your youngster's thought processes. He begins to develop his problem-solving and decision-making skills as he picks colors and materials, works with certain textures and lines, plays with size and shape. He starts to discriminate and differentiate, noticing differences and similarities. He learns about the consequences of events and actions.

By randomly mixing two colors, he has found that white and red make pink. A few days later, he tries again. White and red still yield pink, but by adding more red he gets a darker shade. He selects a wide brush—and paints a wide line. With a slender brush, he produces a thin line. As he assimilates such knowledge, he begins to draw conclusions. In other words, he learns directly from his experience.

Other opportunities for cognitive development abound in the act of creating. A child rolling clay into a ball notes the ball's resemblance to his favorite fruit and makes his first comparison: "My clay is round like an apple." Or drawing a flower to stand for all flowers, he shows his new ability to generalize information and think symbolically.

Other benefits

Creative pursuits can sharpen your youngster's physical abilities as well as her thought processes. Painting sweeping lines with a big brush calls her gross motor skills into play. Producing a detailed picture with a felt-tip pen or cutting out patterns from pieces of construction paper with scissors exercises her developing fine motor skills and helps improve her eye-hand

Old boxes, a roll of masking tape, a lot of ingenuity, and considerable dedication enable this girl to create her own sculpture. She will stop only when she thinks the work is finished.

coordination as well. As children draw, paint, or sculpt, they necessarily examine their environment a little more closely. They begin to notice colors, forms, spatial relationships in it, just as they do in the materials that they are working with. Their powers of perception increase, and they become increasingly aware of aesthetic values. They learn to appreciate beauty. In addition, the practical knowledge that they can attain from their arts and crafts projects will serve them well as they continue to find out how the world works. Although most children, obviously, are not going to grow up to be a Pablo Picasso or a Georgia O'Keeffe, their creativity will help them to see the world with freshness.

Rewards of group activity

Depending on how old she is, your child may enjoy participating in arts and crafts activities with other children, and there are valuable lessons to be learned here too. When they work in groups, children discover what it means to cooperate. Is there only one jar of green tempera? Then perhaps it is best to share it as they are painting a mural. One little girl admires the way another girl makes wavy blue lines to represent the sky. Before long, she will be making lines like that herself—except she will be using them, perhaps, to show how the wind is whipping up waves in a lake.

When the project has been completed, the children must help wash up and put away the brushes and screw the caps on the jars of paint so that it will not dry out. Taking care of art materials teaches a sense of responsibility—and this is an attribute that can carry over into other parts of your child's life.

The joy of art

But in addition to all that children learn from their arts and crafts activities, there is still the sheer, unadulterated, and unbeatable joy of simply doing them. It is this that imbues their work with such large amounts of energy and charm. Picasso is reported to have said, "It took me my whole life to learn to draw like a child." When he spoke of drawing "like a child," of course, the artist meant that it took decades for him to be able to reclaim the open, unselfconscious joy in line and color, and the inborn creativity and power of invention that a young child like yours possesses in delightful abundance. ❖

What Can Your Child Do, When?

Like the unfolding of spring, the blossoming of your child's abilities can be predicted only generally. Some sequences do not vary; in your youngster's creative life, designs will follow scribbles as surely as daffodils follow crocuses. But for flowers and children alike, the timing can vary.

Governed as it is by such individual factors as attention span, coordination, and fine muscle control, the pace of your child's artistic growth cannot be rushed. But you can smooth the way by nurturing his confidence and his love of arts and crafts. The charts on these pages, by framing your youngster's budding artistic skills in the context of his overall development, will help you tailor creative projects to your child's expanding abilities.

Eighteen Months to Three Years

General Characteristics

The toddler stage, from your child's first steps to about his third birthday, is typified by high energy and enormous curiosity. Your youngster eagerly explores everything in every possible way—smelling, tasting, mouthing, stacking, banging, twisting, tearing apart.

His attention span, however, is short; he will not stay independently absorbed or involved in a project for more than three or four minutes without adult interaction. He is easily frustrated and prone to occasional temper tantrums.

Early in this period and—for new projects—throughout it, the child wants adult help and support. He may have periods of whiny indecision, but when he gains confidence about an activity, he will insist on doing it himself.

From twenty-four months on, your youngster's actions are increasingly purposeful; in art, he may try to copy a square or a circle. He learns mostly through imitation and trial-and-error exploration, with some adult direction.

Artistic Skills

- Is fascinated by the physical processes of painting, drawing, and molding; not very interested in the product. Will cheerfully tear or squash own artwork.

- At first holds a marker any way, between stiff fingers or in fist; moves whole arm. Drawing hand does not touch paper; free hand seldom steadies paper. At about two years, holds large marker between thumb and forefinger, uses some wrist action.

- Scribbles randomly, drawing off edges or not filling paper. Also likes to draw on walls, self, other child. In later scribbling, lines, zigzags, circles well defined, sometimes repeated.

- By about two, can crudely copy vertical, horizontal, and curved lines. By three, can do a rough circle.

- Spends less than a minute on a drawing.

- Finger-paints with whole hand.

- Finds painting easier at easel; needs large (½- to ¾-inch) brush.

- By thirty months, names a color.

- Enjoys texture more than color. Paints with any color handy. May be content to use just one; may layer several colors onto paper, then rub them together into a muddy gray-brown.

- Works with clay by squeezing, pounding, pulling—and tasting.

- At two, can make a single scissor-snip; cannot cut a continuous line.

- At two, can fold paper once, imitatively. At two-and-a-half, can fold and crease; at three, can fold and crease horizontally and vertically into uneven rectangle, but cannot fold paper diagonally.

The Three-Year-Old

General Characteristics

As your three-year-old grows calmer and more confident, she becomes more co-operative, outgoing, and social. In her play group she begins learning to share toys and art supplies, to wait her turn, to notice other people's feelings. She feels proud of her finished artwork and delights in recognition and praise.

She likes repetition and predictable routines; likes to do a task, such as cutting, over and over. She can amuse herself without adult input for five or six minutes, perhaps twenty minutes in a favorite activity. She learns both by observing and imitating adults and through adult explanation and instruction. She thinks before acting and can make simple plans and decisions more easily. Her coordination has improved markedly, so she uses less effort and concentration in accomplishing a task.

She enjoys dramatic play, dress-up, and make-believe. With her active, vivid imagination, she may confuse fiction or dreams with reality.

Artistic Skills

- Still likes creative processes but is more goal-oriented, often decides beforehand what to make. Improvises freely as work goes on.

- Learns to hold drawing tools easily, resting hand on paper and using fingers for fine control; steadies paper with free hand. Uses brush easily.

- Can copy a reasonably accurate circle. Draws a square with straight sides but irregular angles. Draws a cross with lines intersecting off-center.

- Spends two minutes on a drawing.

- Names all colors.

- Experiments with color, often painting separate areas without overlaps.

- Can string beads by colors and shapes.

- Pats and rolls clay into snakes, coils, balls, pancakes; enjoys piercing clay, makes holes for details such as eyes.

- Can use scissors to cut sheet of paper in half.

- Enjoys simple printmaking.

- When making collages, often covers earlier work by pasting other bits of paper over it.

- Shows sense of pattern in drawing, painting, collages. Groups and balances lines, geometric shapes, and colors. Experiments with mandala shape.

- Nearing age four, gives names to scribbles, relating marks on paper to objects or events. May draw people; given unfinished drawing of a human head and body, will add at least two body parts without prompting. May draw details that show feelings—such as tears on a face.

The Four-Year-Old

General Characteristics

As a four-year-old, your little one becomes self-assured, energetic, and exuberant. She is talkative and often boastful, sometimes absurdly so. She eagerly tries anything new, relishing fresh sights and sounds, words and ideas, skills and accomplishments. She wants to save her artwork now. She is becoming less self-centered and more cooperative, and her friendships with peers continue to develop. Given the appropriate teaching and guidance, she behaves courteously and obeys simple rules.

She is very active, racing everywhere, welcoming athletic challenges. She likes to work fast. Less distractible now, she may play for twenty minutes without help. Once she begins a task, she can carry it out without constant supervision and usually finishes what she starts.

Constantly asking "how" and "why" questions, she listens closely to the answers. She learns now through observing, questioning, and listening, as well as through exploration.

Artistic Skills

- Uses adult grip for pencils and crayons.

- Draws objects and figures that float in space, without foreground or horizon.

- Draws a recognizable human figure with head, eyes, and legs.

- Spends 2½ minutes on a drawing.

- Finger-paints with enthusiasm, using many motions to achieve effects.

- Chooses colors deliberately, although the effect—purple hair, say—may not match the picture's real model.

- Can tie simple knots; cannot tie shoe. Can thread beads of less than ½-inch diameter onto string.

- Uses blocks to construct buildings, cities. Makes equally elaborate collages, handling paste easily, often planning work in advance.

- Can make three-dimensional mobiles and constructions with pipe cleaners; may need help with connections.

- Makes basic clay forms such as ball, oval, and rectangle, then joins them to create figures. Also may shape a figure from one large piece of clay.

- Can cut long line or curve with scissors, keeping blades from closing completely, turning paper with other hand at same time.

- Accurately folds paper in any direction, aligning the edges.

- Tells stories about own drawings.

- Makes mostly representational art. May start project without result in mind, but ends up depicting real objects in drawings or sculptures. Uses symbols—simplified drawings—for people, trees, houses, flowers, animals.

The Five-Year-Old

General Characteristics

Nearing his fifth birthday, your child has a quiet self-assurance. He has definite right- or left-handedness and good eye-hand coordination; these advances confer confidence about controlling materials and completing tasks.

The five-year-old is at ease playing in groups of other children. He is learning new social skills, such as giving and receiving; he is eager to please, and he understands and obeys rules.

He has grasped the concept of comparison, for such qualities as darker/lighter, heavier/lighter, faster/slower. Similarly, he is able to sort objects by color, shape, or size.

Capable of sustained concentration despite distractions, he can work alone for thirty minutes on average, sometimes up to an hour. He can plan activities and save them for a suitable time and place, perhaps even putting a project aside until the next day.

He continues to learn through experimentation, observation, and questioning.

Artistic Skills

- At start of project, can describe concept, plan, materials, colors. Tends to follow plan purposefully, compare artwork with concept. Will often crumple artwork for tiny flaw.

- Draws skillfully but remains uncertain with diagonals; can copy square but not diamond.

- At first enlarges important details without respect to real size—drawing flower larger than house; later begins to understand proportions and depicts objects in their relative sizes.

- Creates pictures and sculptures modeled literally on familiar objects. Adds details such as hair and fingers, even glasses, earrings, shoelaces. Can draw house with roof, door, windows, chimney, perhaps tree in yard.

- Spends three minutes or more on a single drawing.

- By the age of six, may have own style of drawing people, houses, and other symbols, distinctive in way an adult's handwriting is.

- Mixes paints with sureness and discrimination to make desired hues.

- Threads large needle; sews with yarn.

- Tends to select items to apply to clay (buttons, straws) as planned part of construction rather than for mere satisfaction of sticking things into clay.

- Chooses collage materials thoughtfully, cuts them into interesting shapes, balances one shape with another.

- Makes balanced constructions and collages unassisted. Can join materials with wire, pipe cleaners, yarn, or tape.

- At five, can cut square. By six, clips magazine picture accurately.

Encouraging Creativity

However naturally creative your child may be, you must offer her the opportunity to express herself. Whether you start her out with some of the projects in this book, or with just a couple of crayons and a blank sheet of paper, you will be sending a message: You think creative activities are important, and you value her creativity. But be sure to present a variety of projects and materials so that she can make some real choices. Try, of course, to match the projects to her capabilities. For a younger child, it is wise to focus on simple tasks and bigger tools—fatter crayons, wider brushes, larger pieces of paper. If you are uncertain about precisely where your youngster stands in terms of her creative development, check the chart on pages 10-13, which describes children's readiness for various tasks at different ages. Bear in mind that even if your child is at the right age level for a particular project, she may need to practice her skills first in order to succeed.

A time and a place

What is the best time and place for you to encourage your youngster's creativity? Perhaps most important is to make creative activities a regular part of your youngster's daily routine, which will give her time to become comfortable with various art materials—squeezing, dripping, swirling them—before she can start using them to express herself fully. The best time for doing this is when she is ready—when she does not feel hungry or thirsty or sleepy or sick or restless. You might also want to alternate active and quiet projects. A child who has spent most of the day outdoors with other children might welcome a quiet time to work on crafts. On the other hand, if she has spent hours indoors, she might prefer to hike through the neighborhood, hunting down dried leaves and seeds for a collage.

The best place for doing projects is a spot where it is okay to be messy, and from which you have removed distractions such as a loud TV. You need not devote a special area of your house to arts and crafts. Your kitchen, with its ready supply of running water and its table and other surfaces that can be easily cleaned, is as good a location as any. If your child prefers to work without having to put everything away when you set the table for family meals, you might put an old coffee table in her room. She can sit at it on a child-sized chair, or kneel comfortably on the floor while she works, and she will still have plenty of space for spreading out paper and supplies. When she wants to paint, simply cover the table and floor with plastic and give her a dishpan of soapy water and a sponge that she can use to help you clean up any spills.

Buying materials

As her mother reads nearby, a little girl colors a cardboard box. Children will work longer at creative projects when an adult is present, regardless of how uninvolved the adult may seem to be.

No doubt you will want to give your child a variety of materials to encourage his art activities. The range of items available in arts and crafts stores can dazzle and confuse. But you need not feel compelled to provide him with the latest gimmick or gadget, or more supplies than he can reasonably be expected to use and enjoy. Keep in mind that the selection of materials is not nearly so important as the opportunity to explore the possibilities of any one item freely; your youngster can be just as creative with homemade modeling dough as with imported clay. All the same, choose good-quality brushes, scissors, and other supplies that you know your youngster will be using often. A brush that loses hairs as he draws it across the paper or scissors that tear rather than cut will be as frustrating for a youngster as for an adult.

When you shop, proceed with an eye to safety. Check labels of paints and other materials to be sure that they are nontoxic; and of course you will want to avoid sharp objects, including needles and pins, with which a young child might hurt himself. Before making your choice, take into account your youngster's age and development. You will not want to give him a permanent marker or even clay if he is going to put it in his mouth. Instead, give him a thick crayon or two and save the modeling projects for later.

Just how much should you involve yourself in your child's creative efforts? Unfortunately, there are no set rules. However, research has shown that when an adult is around, children spend nearly twice as much time on a painting or drawing project as they would in the absence of an adult.

You can best help your child by striking a balance between guiding him and giving him freedom. You want your child to develop the confidence and independence to create. His confidence will grow when he feels free to find his own solutions. Let him work without interruptions, and offer help only if requested. Refrain from telling him what you think are the ingredients of a "pretty picture." The child who does not have to worry about pleasing someone else or about turning out a "perfect" finished product will plunge into a project more readily.

Often, your presence is all that is required to maximize your child's involvement. If, for example, he works at a project while you read or do chores nearby, your nonintrusiveness shows confidence in his ability to carry on alone, while your on-call status signals your availability to help out if needed.

A matter of difference Children, even young ones, may develop very strong likes and dislikes. One child may hate a certain color. Another may focus on a single subject for a while, depicting nothing but people, for example, or flowers. Accept the fact that your youngster's tastes and ideas may differ from yours.

Originality is the essence of the creative process. Your child should be able to take chances mixing colors, investigating textures, using different tools. By inventing solutions, she will come to rely on herself for ideas. Even when your child uses step-by-step instructions for a crafts project, she can modify them as her ideas dictate. For example, she can select her favorite colors for the light catcher on page 105. Or she can decorate the costumes and hats on pages 47 to 59 as she likes.

In praise of praise Once you have launched your child on a creative project, be prepared to support him in it. Accentuate the positive when reacting to something that he has produced. Instead of making vague remarks like, "Oh, how pretty!" comment on specifics. You might, for example, praise the combination of colors or the balance of the design. This kind of appreciation instructs as well as compliments. While you should try to find something good in every effort, you should offer favorable comments only if you mean them. Children are quick to pick up on insincerity, and phony praise may do more harm than good.

When your child shows you a picture or presents you with a vaguely modeled lump of clay, do not put him on the spot by asking, "What is it?" Instead, draw him out by saying something like, "Tell me about it." In children, especially, creativity is an ongoing process; one expert likens seeing a child's art to viewing the last frame of a movie. The story the artist tells you about his work will most likely be a marvel of inventiveness and inspire him to create a sequel.

When enough is enough No matter how engrossing a craft activity may be for your young one, the time will come when she says she is finished. What looks unfinished to you may well be complete in her view, and you should respect her judgment; otherwise, she may resist such activities in the future. Keep in mind the possibility that she may have stopped not because she is actually finished, but because she is frustrated. Doubtlessly, she will show signs of her frustration, such as irritation or restlessness. When she does, try to scale down the activity to reflect the level of her skills. She may also have simply run out of ideas. Help her to come up with new ones. For example, you might give her a smaller brush to make different kinds of strokes, or persuade her to continue a picture by asking some leading questions: "What colors would look nice with those colors? What would happen if you tried using the flat end of the crayon instead of the point?"

Children love to have their finished artwork displayed. A miniature gallery may already be affixed with magnets to your refrigerator door. You can also use nonstick masking tape or the nonstaining, puttylike adhesive available in many stores to post pictures on walls. Let your youngster help select the works for display.

Occasionally, you will want to preserve a particularly charming or meaningful example of your child's art in a more permanent way. Her painting or drawing will last longer if it is on sturdy paper high in rag content, rather than on cheaper paper made from wood pulp. You may also want to frame one of her works; this can be done inexpensively using dime-store frames. You can preserve clay objects, once they are dry, by painting them with shellac. While it is important to keep and display certain creations that you and your child have chosen together, do not overdo it lest she lose her spontaneity.

When you appreciate and encourage your child's creativity, you enable her to explore new aesthetic dimensions and widen her horizons. You do not have to be an art expert or even particularly creative yourself to be part of the process. Simply as a result of making it possible for your youngster to express herself, you will see her self-confidence and sense of accomplishment grow. Join her in the process of discovery, and your own skills and interests may grow too. Best of all, the two of you will share and enjoy the fun. ∴

Protected from paint splatters by a smock, a girl works thoughtfully on a colorful painting. Her mother recognizes her efforts (left) by displaying the work on the refrigerator door, thus bolstering the child's self-confidence.

A Cornucopia of Arts and Crafts

The arts and crafts projects that are presented on the following pages are not intended to nurture budding Michelangelos or to teach hand-eye coordination or draftsmanship. Their purpose is simply to let your child develop his innate creativity, in whatever way pleases him. He will learn, among other things, to manipulate paper, paint, and clay, building confidence and a sense of accomplishment as his skills grow. In the process he will be bringing his imagination into full play. The costume on the four-year-old opposite, for example, is made from a box, some plastic drainpipe, a bucket, and a cardboard cylinder. The delightful result is anyone's guess: a robot, a spaceman, a knight-errant, perhaps all three. His pleasure in it is immense.

This chapter is divided into five categories: paper constructions, including collages, origami, flowers, and jewelry; drawing, painting, and printmaking; found objects, or everyday items, used for costumes, castles, dollhouses, and puppets; sculptures made from clay, laundry soap, and papier-mâché; and fabric activities such as weaving and tie-dying. Each section introduction provides general information about materials and techniques.

The projects themselves vary in complexity. Each set of instructions contains a suggested age range, which is intended only as a guideline; you are the best judge of your child's unique needs and abilities. Where adult participation is required, you will find a note to that effect. The illustrated instructions themselves are written in direct address and in simple language. Obviously, since your child is too young to read the instructions, you will have to read them or interpret them for him. But let your child deviate from the instructions as he sees fit. He, after all, is the creator.

No matter how simple the project, you will need to exercise some supervision, not only to ensure safety, but also to intervene if your child becomes frustrated.

Working with Paper

Plentiful, colorful, and easy to manipulate, paper is an ideal medium for young artists. It lends itself to pasting, cutting, and folding, techniques your child will easily master as she matures. Using her newfound skills with occasional guidance from you, she can carry out the suitable projects on the following pages.

Tearing and Pasting. Your toddler's penchant for tearing pieces of paper means that a collage is a natural early project for her. All she needs to do is rip colorful paper into small pieces and then stick them down on a larger sheet. To get her started, clip pages from magazines or the Sunday funnies, and let her go to town on them. If she feels uncomfortable about tearing paper—as do some youngsters who have been taught that tearing is wrong—you can cut out some small pieces for her to paste.

When introducing your youngster to pasting, you can minimize mess by using the kind of thick paste that comes in a jar with a brush attached to the lid. Lacking that, get a one-half-inch-wide paintbrush, shorten its handle to four or five inches, put some paste in a nonbreakable bowl, and have her dip into it. Demonstrate how to use the paste by brushing a little onto the background sheet and placing a torn piece of paper on top. As she becomes more skilled, you can show her how to apply the glue to the piece itself, but be patient—a beginner is as likely to glue the torn paper to herself as to the background sheet.

Using Scissors. Introduce paper cutting after your little one has worked successfully with paste a few times. Choose well-made, four- to six-inch blunt-nosed safety scissors, which are available for both right- and left-handed children. For her first tries at cutting, give her narrow strips of paper that she can cut crosswise with single snips. Beginners also enjoy making fringes.

Later you can show your youngster how to cut a long piece of paper by holding the scissors in one place to operate them and sliding the paper into the scissors with her other hand. If she finds the scissors hard to control, show her how she can rest the edge of the bottom of the scissors on the table as she opens and closes the blades.

Since cutting requires considerable coordination and concentration, provide your youngster with opportunities to improve her skill. Cutting a straight line is difficult; in fact, it may be impossible for children younger than the age of four; you should precut any pieces that require such precision. Give your child medium-weight shelf paper or butcher paper for practice; these are easier to control than tissue paper and easier to cut than construction paper.

Folding Paper. As with cutting, start with simple steps. You can begin by showing your child how to fold a sheet of paper in half, explaining to her how the edges should come together. Then have her press down the crease. Give her a few sheets of paper to fold in half, but do not expect her to succeed perfectly.

Making single-fold greeting cards with pictures cut from magazines is a satisfying project for a beginner. The fold-and-cut projects on pages 22-23 take into account your youngster's abilities. The more challenging origami activities on pages 26-27 will work even if your child still has trouble bringing edges together.

When your youngster is ready for it, have her produce her own book. The project is fun to do, and it will call her pasting, cutting, and folding skills into play. To start, all she has to do is fold several sheets of paper in half and staple them between construction-paper covers. In time, your child will want a greater challenge. A four-year-old, for example, can master the skills required to decorate the covers, employing a marbling technique *(pages 29-30)* that has been used for centuries by master bookbinders.

Choosing Adhesives

Adhesives come in a number of forms, suitable for a variety of projects and skill levels.

- Library paste, which is spillproof, is good for beginners. Flour paste—made by stirring ½ cup of flour into ⅔ cup of water—is a workable substitute.

- Nontoxic white glue in a plastic squeeze bottle is excellent for more experienced preschoolers. Have your youngster use a small bottle that you can refill. Or, to minimize waste, pour some glue into a small bowl and have her apply it with a brush.

- Nontoxic glue stick is a more expensive but less messy adhesive.

Paper-Strip Sculpture

Ages 3 to 6

Paper can be used to create striking
three-dimensional designs.

Cut strips of various lengths from pieces of colored
construction paper. Put a little paste or glue on one
end of a strip and attach that end to a sheet of paper,
pressing it with your finger for a few seconds before
letting go. Form the strip into an arch, a pinched
peak, accordion folds, or a twist, and paste the other
end to the large sheet of construction paper. Repeat
this process with the other strips.

Crumpled-Tissue Collage

Ages 2 to 5

Tissue paper, which tears and crumples
easily, is an ideal medium for collage.

Crumple 2- to 4-inch squares of colored tissue paper
into balls. Dab one side of each ball with white glue,
or dip it in the adhesive, and stick it onto construction
paper. Toddlers may wind up enjoying playing with
the glue more than making the collage; younger
preschoolers may simply cram their sheets with as
many paper balls as possible; older preschoolers may
make designs, using various colors.

Revolving Spirals

Suspended over a warm air current,
the spiral will spin lazily.

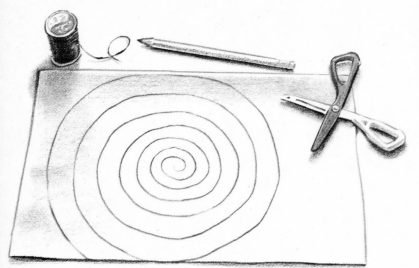

*A spiral cut from light cardboard or stiff paper—a
gift-box lid works well, as does a large Christmas
card—and hung by a thread with a knot at the end, to
keep it from slipping out, is fun to make and to watch
twirl. For a two-tone spiral, glue a sheet of colored
construction paper to the cardboard before drawing
and cutting out the spiral.*

Simple Cut-Paper Designs

Ages 3 to 4
Gluing the designs to colored
backgrounds enhances them.

*Fold a piece of typing paper or other medium-
weight paper in half and then in half again, forming
quarters. Randomly clip pieces from the corners
and the edges of the folded sheet. Unfold the paper
carefully to reveal the cutout design.*

Lacy Doilies

Ages 4 to 6

A more intricate folding and cutting project than the simple cut-paper design shown at the bottom of the opposite page, this cutout begins with a lesson in squaring a rectangular piece of paper.

Materials

typing paper
scissors
colored construction paper
glue

1

To make a square from a rectangular piece of paper, first make a triangle by folding the paper diagonally so that a short side meets a long side evenly. Cut away the strip next to the triangle (right), then open the triangle.

2

Fold the square into quarters (below). Then fold the resulting square diagonally, forming another triangle. Halve the triangle by folding its opposite corners together (below, right).

3

Snip pieces from the edges and corners. The more cuts, the lacier the square will be. Open gently so as not to tear. Mount the doily on a sheet of construction paper (top).

Paper-Bead Necklace

Ages 4 to 6

Materials

typing or drawing paper
pencil
scissors
glue in a small plastic bowl
liquid tempera paint
paintbrush
yarn
masking tape

1

Begin by marking and then cutting out paper rectangles, each of them 1½ inches by 5 inches. A child's necklace takes ten or more rectangles.

2

Dip a rectangle into the glue, covering it on both sides. Let the excess glue drip off into the bowl; or strip off the glue by using one hand to gently pull the paper up between two fingers of your free hand.

3

Lay a short end of the rectangle on a pencil, and make a bead by rolling the paper around the pencil (right). Slip the bead off and set it, flap down, on wax paper to dry overnight. Repeat Steps 2 and 3 for each of the remaining rectangles.

4

After the beads have dried completely, paint them with liquid tempera. Lay the painted beads on a smooth surface. Wait an hour or so for the beads to dry thoroughly before stringing them.

5

Wrap one end of the yarn with masking tape, for easy stringing. Then string the beads onto the yarn (right). Remove the tape, and then tie the two ends of the yarn together.

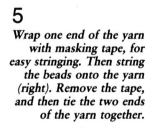

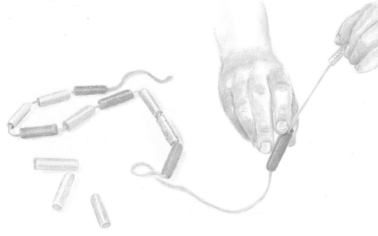

Origami Drinking Cup

Ages 5 to 6
Adult participation required

This easy-to-make paper cup will actually hold cold liquids long enough for a sip or toast.

Materials
origami paper, 5¾ inches square (or colored wrapping paper with a white side, cut to size)

1

With the white side of the paper facing up and the sheet angled to form a diamond, fold the lower corner to the upper corner, creating a colored triangle. Crease the folds.

2

To begin making the left side of the cup, fold the left corner of the triangle over to the middle of the right side. Crease.

3

Construct the right side of the cup by folding the bottom right corner over to the upper left corner of the triangle you formed in Step 2. The paper is now symmetrical again.

4

Fold the facing upper flap down, revealing its white side. Turn the cup over and repeat the same step with the second flap. To open the cup, gently squeeze the two upper corners toward the center.

26

Origami Sailboat

Ages 5 to 6

Here is a boat that will not float but can be displayed on a shelf or table.

Materials

origami paper, 5¾ inches square (or colored wrapping paper with a white side, cut to size)

safety scissors

1

Cut the square into two triangles. Lay one white side up. Bring the opposite corners together, crease along the center, and unfold (left).

2

With the long side toward you, fold the top point down to where the crease meets the bottom edge so the colored side of the paper is visible (below).

3

Fold the left triangle up along the left edge of the middle triangle and make a crease (left).

4

Form a colored diamond by folding the right triangle up along the right edge of the middle triangle (left); make a crease.

5

Bring the bottom point up to the center (above); crease and then unfold it to form a base. Turn the boat around, resting it on the base (top).

Mexican Flowers

Ages 4 to 6
Adult participation required

Materials
tissue paper in five colors
paper clip
plate 4 to 6 inches in diameter
pencil
safety scissors
pipe cleaners

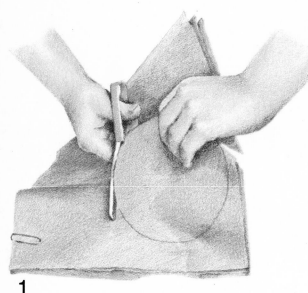

1
*Clip together a stack of
five sheets of tissue paper,
each a different color. Lay
the plate face down on the
paper and trace its outline;
following this outline,
cut a circle out, through all
five layers (above).*

2
*With a pencil point, poke
two holes to either side of
the circle's center, making
sure to pierce all five
layers. Bend a pipe cleaner
in half, push one end
through each hole, and
twist the ends together
(below) into a stem.*

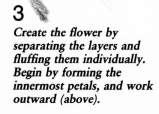

3
*Create the flower by
separating the layers and
fluffing them individually.
Begin by forming the
innermost petals, and work
outward (above).*

Marbled Accordion Book

Ages 4 to 6

Adult participation required

With adult assistance, a preschooler can make marbled covers for a book of his own.

Materials

For the marbled paper

water
cornstarch
liquid dish detergent
liquid tempera paint
1-inch-wide paintbrush
toothbrush
drawing paper, 4¼ by 9 inches
newspaper

For the book

two pieces of posterboard, 3⅛ inches square
drawing paper, 3 by 18 inches
two pieces of marbled paper *(instructions below)*
narrow fabric ribbon, 24 inches long
safety scissors
glue
½-inch-wide paintbrush
wax paper

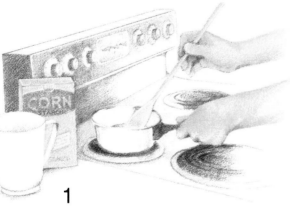

1
Combine 1 tablespoon of cold water with 1 tablespoon of cornstarch and add the mixture to 9 tablespoons water boiling in a saucepan. Stir it until the mixture turns translucent (a minute or two) and remove from the heat. Add ⅛ teaspoon of liquid dish detergent and let the mixture cool. Stir in 2 tablespoons of tempera.

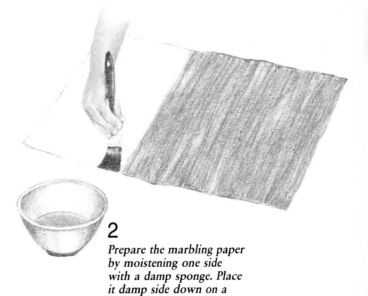

2
Prepare the marbling paper by moistening one side with a damp sponge. Place it damp side down on a pad of newspapers, then smooth it flat. Use the paintbrush to coat the paper with the colored paste (above).

3

Using the toothbrush, swirl patterns in the paste; you might make regular scallops (right) or a more free-form design. Let the paper dry overnight; then cut out two squares, each 4½ inches on a side.

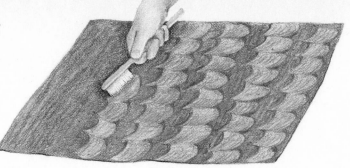

4

To begin assembling a cover, lay the decorated side of one square down on a work surface. Now brush glue on one side of a posterboard square and center it, glue side down, on the back of the marbled paper (right), pressing to make it stick.

5

Put glue on each corner of the paper and fold it over the posterboard, forming triangles (above). Then glue and fold each remaining edge over the posterboard (above, right). Repeat Steps 4 and 5 with the other posterboard and marbled paper.

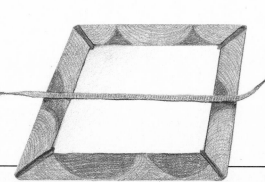

6

Brush a line of glue across the middle of one completed cover, and set the ribbon in the glue.

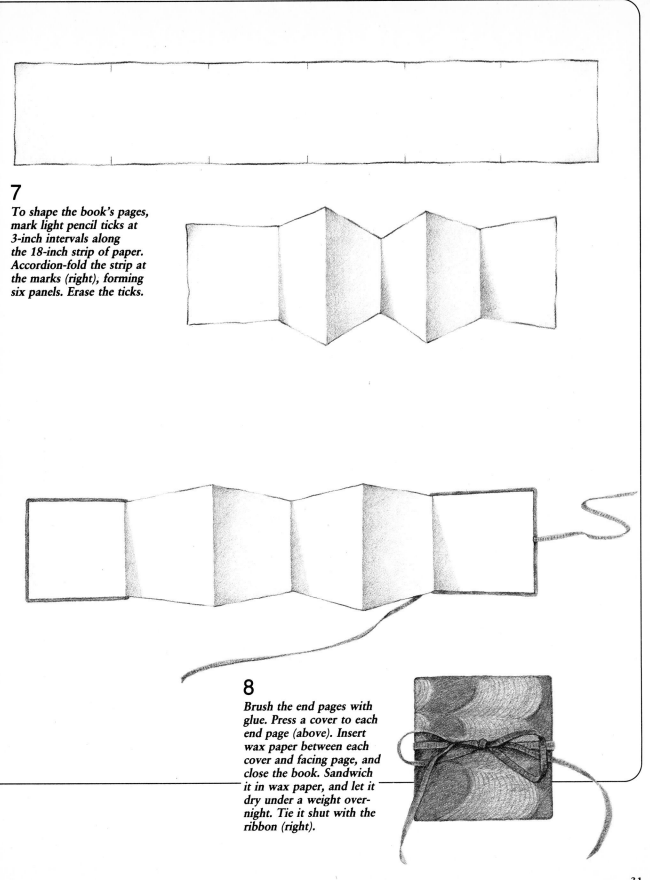

7

To shape the book's pages, mark light pencil ticks at 3-inch intervals along the 18-inch strip of paper. Accordion-fold the strip at the marks (right), forming six panels. Erase the ticks.

8

Brush the end pages with glue. Press a cover to each end page (above). Insert wax paper between each cover and facing page, and close the book. Sandwich it in wax paper, and let it dry under a weight overnight. Tie it shut with the ribbon (right).

Painting, Drawing, and Printing

Children delight in using colors freely on paper, but a child has a short attention span, and you may need a little ingenuity from time to time to keep up your youngster's enthusiasm. One of the best ways is to maintain a well-stocked supply cabinet and a mental list of interesting projects. The practical suggestions for making or assembling supplies and the various activities offered on the pages that follow are designed to help you get your child involved in a range of creative endeavors.

Paper. Almost any kind of paper may be used—from grocery bags to an occasional piece of high-quality bond. Inexpensive newsprint is fine for drawing with crayons and markers. For painting or printing, try heavier sixty-pound-weight manila or white drawing paper. Whatever the type, choose large sheets. Rolls of coated shelf paper, an economical substitute for special finger-paint paper, are ideal for finger painting and murals.

Crayons, Chalk, and Markers. Thick crayons hold up best in little fingers. To recycle broken ones into rainbow disks that can be used to striking effect, put a few old crayons of different colors—paper removed—into one or more cups of a muffin tin. Preheat the oven to 325° F. and turn it off. Put the pan in the oven just until the wax melts and the colors fuse—about two minutes. Let cool, then pop the disks out.

Wash the pan in very hot water to get rid of waxy residue.

Wide, soft colored chalk is perfect for drawing on chalkboards and sidewalks, and youngsters love to use it on dark, textured paper as well. To keep the chalk from rubbing off paper, apply hairspray when the drawing is done.

Brightly colored felt-tip markers should also be among a child's art supplies. Buy the nontoxic, water-based kind.

Paint and Brushes. Water-soluble tempera paint is good for children's projects. It comes in premixed liquid form and in powder, which is cheaper but tricky to mix. If you buy the premixed variety, add a squeeze of liquid dish detergent to each jar. (The detergent makes the paint easier to apply and clean up; it also permits the paint to adhere to milk cartons and other waxy surfaces.) If you buy the powder, prepare it yourself to avoid the risk of your child's inhaling particles or spilling paint. Add one part powder to two parts detergent and two parts water. Let it sit for a few minutes, then stir gently. It should be the consistency of heavy cream.

You can create your own finger paint by combining two tablespoons of cornstarch and six tablespoons of cold water and stirring the mixture into one-half cup of boiling water in a pan set over medium-high heat. Stir until the mixture thickens—two to three minutes. Remove the mixture from the heat, and add tempera or food coloring to it.

As your child's skills develop, she may appreciate the

How to Minimize Mess and Make Cleaning Up Easy

A few simple precautions can save hours cleaning up after junior painters. If you set aside a special work area where spills will do no serious damage and follow the practical tips below, you can allow your little one to explore paint's many possibilities without having to worry about messes.

- **Protecting surfaces.** Never let your youngster paint or print on a floor or table that can be stained or otherwise permanently damaged. Cover it with an old plastic tablecloth or shower curtain, or an inexpensive plastic drop cloth. Newspapers will do, but since they readily absorb moisture, you may find yourself later washing off smudges left by the damp paper.

- **Paint cleanup.** Guard against spills by filling containers

halfway. If you have added liquid detergent to your tempera, you will have a creamy paint that wipes up easily.

- **A homemade coverall.** A discarded man's shirt can easily be a full-length smock for a small child. To keep long sleeves from getting in the way, cut them off at your youngster's elbows. If the shirt trails to the floor, shorten it so he will not trip. Put the shirt on the child backward and button it down the back. You can encourage clean hands by attaching an old hand towel to the portion of the smock that covers your youngster's chest.

- **Keeping sponges handy.** A damp sponge kept next to your young artist's brush-cleaning bowl will make it easy for her to wipe off newly rinsed brushes.

subtleties of watercolors. A tin of semimoist paints and a couple of good brushes are expensive but far more rewarding to use than cheaper ones. Show her how to rinse and wipe her brush on a paper towel whenever she changes colors. By varying the amount of water she mixes with the paint or by lightly sponging the paper before painting, she can create different effects.

Fat brushes with half-inch- to inch-wide bristles and four- to five-inch handles are easiest for small children to wield. As your child grows older, add thinner brushes as well. After use, rinse each brush carefully and store it upright in a jar so that the bristles will air-dry and keep their shape.

Printing Supplies. Water-based printer's ink, in tubes, is best for printing projects. Or make your own by combining equal parts of tempera powder and premixed wallpaper paste. Rubber ink rollers, or brayers, available at art supply stores, are worthwhile if your youngster is especially interested in printing. To prepare the brayer for printing, squeeze an inch or two of printer's ink onto a washable work surface or a cookie sheet, and roll the brayer through it until it is thoroughly coated. But if your child is merely experimenting with shapes, using cut vegetables and sponges *(page 40),* she will need an inkpad, which you can easily provide by lining an aluminum pie plate with several thicknesses of paper towels and adding a few tablespoons of tempera paint.

Introducing Toddlers to Paint

A paintbrush, a bucket of water, and a sidewalk on a warm summer afternoon can offer your toddler an ideal introduction to painting. She will have the thrill of creating new patterns without any mess.

When she is ready to explore painting further, give her a large sheet of paper, a wide brush, and a few spoonfuls of tempera paint in a stable bowl. Briefly show her how to put the paint on the brush and on the paper and then let her explore from there.

Many toddlers prefer fingers to brushes and will smear finger paints around with great gusto. Show your child how to spread the paint with her fingertips or the sides of her hands. Do not be surprised if she discovers that elbows work equally well. If she feels uncomfortable with the gooey consistency of finger paint, give her a flat stick to use as a tool *(page 36)*. For a less sticky paint, squeeze a bit of liquid detergent on her paper, add a drop of food coloring to it— and then let her go to town. You might also have her finger-paint in the bathtub, giving her some tempera mixed with liquid dish detergent or commercially made soap paint.

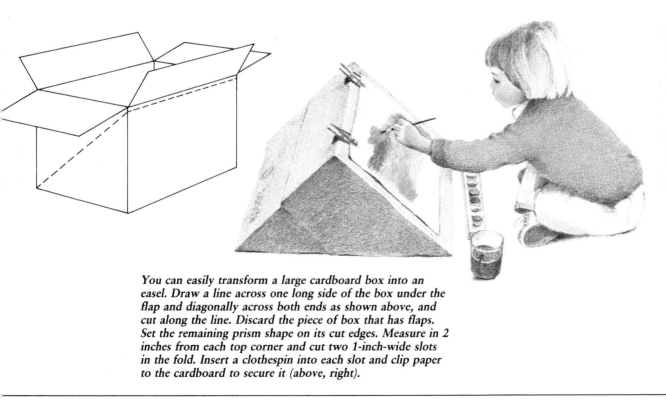

You can easily transform a large cardboard box into an easel. Draw a line across one long side of the box under the flap and diagonally across both ends as shown above, and cut along the line. Discard the piece of box that has flaps. Set the remaining prism shape on its cut edges. Measure in 2 inches from each top corner and cut two 1-inch-wide slots in the fold. Insert a clothespin into each slot and clip paper to the cardboard to secure it (above, right).

Exploring Color

As your toddler approaches school age, her interest in drawing and painting will broaden. Whereas just a few months ago she was content to happily scribble away with a single crayon, now she is enthralled by having several colors to choose from. The activities described here and on the following pages should stimulate her exciting new interest by helping her to discover the myriad combinations she can create out of just black, white, and the three primary colors—red, yellow, blue.

Running colors together. Children often learn quite by accident how colors magically transform themselves when they flow into each other. For example, while a child is painting a blue sky around a yellow sun, the colors may, without her intending it, "bleed" to create a green halo.

It is easy to give your youngster the opportunity to experiment with such happy accidents. First, put a tablespoon each of white, red, yellow, and blue paint into separate small bowls. Add a little water to thin each paint to a runny consistency. Next, tape a sheet of paper inside the lid of a gift box. Have your child drop a teaspoon or two of each color onto different areas of the paper, and then rock the lid from side to side so that the colors run together. Or, as an alternative mixing technique, drop a marble into the lid and let it roll around. The two of you can play "color detective." Start at a newly formed color, such

Paint-Mixing Tips

- A small child can be overwhelmed by too many choices. Until your beginning painter becomes accustomed to mixing paints, limit the number of colors he works with to four at any one time, preferably black, white, and two others. After a few sessions, he can expand his repertoire.

- The type of paper you supply will affect the color of the paint your youngster applies. A bright red tempera, for example, may appear brick red on a brown paper bag but fiery orange on yellow construction paper. And light-colored paint will be more vivid if it is used on a dark sheet. To demonstrate this dramatic effect, have your child paint half a sheet of white paper gray, then paint over the entire sheet with another color. Afterward, he can compare the two halves and see the difference the gray undercoat makes.

- Arrange paler shades of paint closest to your child to encourage him to use these colors first, providing a light base for his work.

- When you buy meat, save the small plastic-foam tray it comes in, wash it clean, and let your child use it for mixing paints. When he mixes, have him start with lighter colors and add the darker ones a bit at a time until he has the shade he desires.

This little girl is learning about color changes from a color sampler made out of three pieces of tinted acetate, a see-through, cellophane-like material that can be purchased at art and drafting supply stores. As the samples overlap, they produce different colors.

as purple, and find the paths of red and blue that lead back to the original drops of paint.

Blending Colors. All your child needs to conduct his own color experiments are different food dyes, water, clear plastic cups, and a medicine dropper. It is a good idea to keep an empty bowl and a fresh water supply nearby so you can pour off murky water and replace it with clean from time to time.

First, half-fill nine or ten one-ounce clear plastic cups with water. (These cups, which are available at party supply stores, allow your preschooler to have fun mixing colors without wasting large quantities of dye or risking major spills.) Have him put several drops of red, yellow, and blue into three separate cups, pointing out how the color of the water intensifies as he adds each drop. Show him how to clean out the dropper with clear water before dipping it into another color. When the colors seem strong enough, suggest that he use the dropper now to mix some red and blue water he has made in a cup of clear water. Talk with him about how the resulting color, purple, changes its hue with each additional drop of red or blue. Repeat the experiment, first using red and yellow, then blue and yellow. When he is through, suggest that he mix the leftover colors a few drops at a time. By adding bright red to dark green, for example, he can create brown.

Your child will enjoy making similar discoveries using home-made modeling dough *(recipe, page 80)* that he colors himself. Have him divide the dough into three lumps, poke a hole in each with his finger, and then squeeze two or three drops of red food coloring into the first hole, yellow into the second, and blue into the third. Your child should then cover the holes with dough and knead each piece until the color is distributed throughout. By taking small bits of different-colored dough and working them together in his hand, he can create a host of interesting color combinations.

Taking a Color Walk. As you and your little one stroll through your neighborhood, ask him to look closely at the colors of various sights that catch his eye. Explain that few objects are one color only. He may notice, for example, that the sky appears as an endless number of subtle blues, greys, and whites. When you return home, suggest that he try his hand at creating shades similar to those he observed by adding white and black paint to a color of his choice. This activity will help him to understand that a single color can vary enormously depending on how much black or white is added.

Colorful Moods. As older preschoolers become more aware of color, they may begin to associate certain colors with certain emotions. If your child is at this stage, now is the time to try an interesting exercise. Give him several tempera paints, including black and white, and have him dampen a large sheet of paper with a wet sponge. Play a lively recording and ask him to brush "happy" colors on the sheet. The dampened paper will cause the colors to merge, creating additional combinations. Then give him a second sheet of paper and play a lullaby or a more solemn piece of music; have him react to the music by painting again. Afterward, you might want to talk together about the differences.

How to Make a Color Wheel

A color wheel is a traditional tool for demonstrating how colors relate to one another. To make the simple one shown here, draw a circle on a sheet of white paper and divide it into six equal wedges. Ask your preschooler to paint the wedges with tempera or with watercolors, which show up well on paper because of their transparency. She should paint every other wedge with a primary color: first red, then yellow, then blue. Now have her mix red with yellow, blue with yellow, and red with blue to get orange, green, and purple respectively. Tell her to fill in the blank wedges with the new colors, placing them between the two colors from which they sprang.

Your child can use the finished product to explore the effect of combining the so-called complementary colors—those opposite each other on the wheel. Suggest, for example, that she mix red and green, or blue and orange. She will soon discover that any pair of complementary colors makes brown.

Cup Painting

You can substitute another object for the plastic cup used here.

Pour a teaspoonful of liquid tempera paint on a sheet of coated stock paper, such as shelf or finger-paint paper. Instead of a brush, use a flat-bottomed plastic cup, spiraling its cup bottom across the paper, pressing down on it to leave an impression, or using the cup's sides as a roller to spread the paint. If you add a color, first clean the cup with a damp sponge.

Painting with Paste

Ages 2 to 3

This activity can serve as a delightful substitute for finger painting.

Several teaspoonfuls of flour, a few drops of food coloring, and a little water mixed together make a colorful paste. Put a spoonful on a piece of paper and draw in it with an ice-cream stick or a tongue depressor. The paste's thick consistency will add a new dimension to the painting experience.

Stick and Sparkle

Ages 4 to 6

Use nonmetallic glitter. The metallic version adheres to sticky little fingers and if rubbed into the eyes can cause damage.

Materials

white glue
liquid tempera paint
plastic bowls
teaspoons
construction paper
nonmetallic glitter in dispenser

1

Make sticky paint in different colors by stirring together equal amounts of glue and paint in several bowls, one bowl per color.

2

Using a fresh spoon each time, scoop a teaspoon of paint from each bowl and dribble the different colors across the paper in patterns. Use the spoon to swirl the paint about.

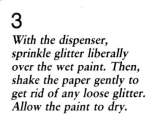

3

With the dispenser, sprinkle glitter liberally over the wet paint. Then, shake the paper gently to get rid of any loose glitter. Allow the paint to dry.

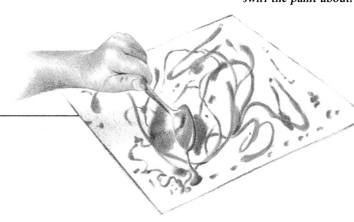

Sandpaper Drawing

Ages 3 to 6

For this exercise in textures,
coarse-grained sandpaper works best.

*Glue a sheet of sandpaper to an 8½-by-11-inch piece
of cardboard. Attach a sheet of typing paper or other
lightweight bond to the sandpaper with a paper clip.
When you draw on the paper, the grainy texture
underneath will lend the work a special look.*

Foot Painting

Ages 3 to 6

This amusing but messy activity is best
done outdoors.

*Spread a large sheet of freezer paper or postal wrap
on the ground, anchoring it, if you wish, with
masking tape. Pour liquid starch into a large, shallow
pan to a depth of ¼ inch and stir in a spoonful of
tempera paint. Sit on a small chair, with the pan to
the side and the paper in front of you, and dip your
feet in the paint, then put your feet on the paper and
paint with them. Keep a towel and a second pan filled
with water and detergent handy for cleaning.*

Chalk Drawing

Ages 3 to 6

Milk contains a natural fixative called casein, used by artists for centuries.

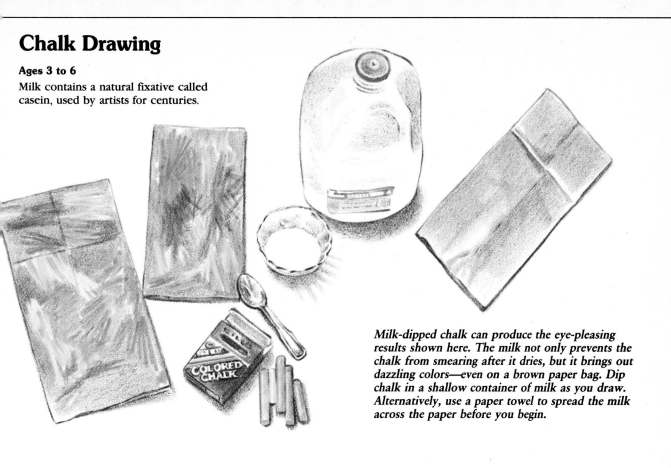

Milk-dipped chalk can produce the eye-pleasing results shown here. The milk not only prevents the chalk from smearing after it dries, but it brings out dazzling colors—even on a brown paper bag. Dip chalk in a shallow container of milk as you draw. Alternatively, use a paper towel to spread the milk across the paper before you begin.

Drip Painting

Ages 4 to 6

Adult participation required

The medicine droppers called for here can be bought at a drug store.

Thin a small amount of tempera paint with water and apply it to paper with medicine droppers. The result will be an attractive abstract painting like this one. To enhance the effect of the thinned paint, dampen the paper with a wet sponge before you begin the dripping. As the paint hits the wet surface, the colors will swirl in lively patterns.

Kitchen Printing

Ages 3 to 6
Adult participation required

To produce prints like those below, slice fruits and vegetables such as apples, broccoli, green peppers, and mushrooms in half lengthwise, or cut sponges into simple shapes. Line aluminum pie plates with paper towels; soak the towels with liquid tempera mixed with a few drops of dishwashing detergent. Rub the fruits, vegetables, or sponges in the towels and press them gently onto paper to make designs.

Crayon Transfer

Ages 5 to 6

Materials

crayons
thin tracing or typing paper
pencil

1

To make a transfer sheet, coat a piece of paper thoroughly with different crayon colors, pressing down heavily.

2

Lay the crayoned transfer sheet face down on a clean piece of paper. Pressing heavily on a pencil, draw a picture on the back of the transfer sheet.

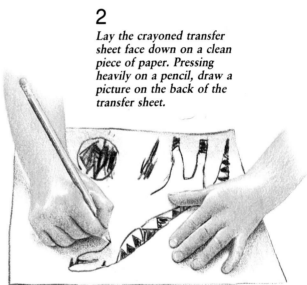

3

Separate the two sheets carefully to reveal the multicolored image of the drawing on the underlying sheet of paper.

Plastic-Foam Printing

Ages 4 to 6
Brayers, or rollers, and tubes of
water-based printer's ink are available
at art supply stores.

Materials
plastic-foam meat tray
safety scissors
ballpoint pen
water-based printer's ink
aluminum baking pan
brayer
medium-weight paper

1

*Cut off the sides of the
plastic-foam tray with
scissors. Then, pressing
down firmly on a ballpoint
pen, draw a picture or
design (below) on the foam
to make a template.*

2

*Squeeze two inches of
ink into the baking dish.
Roll the brayer back and
forth in the ink (below)
until it is evenly coated.*

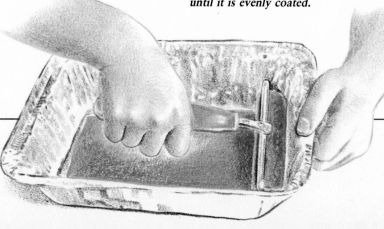

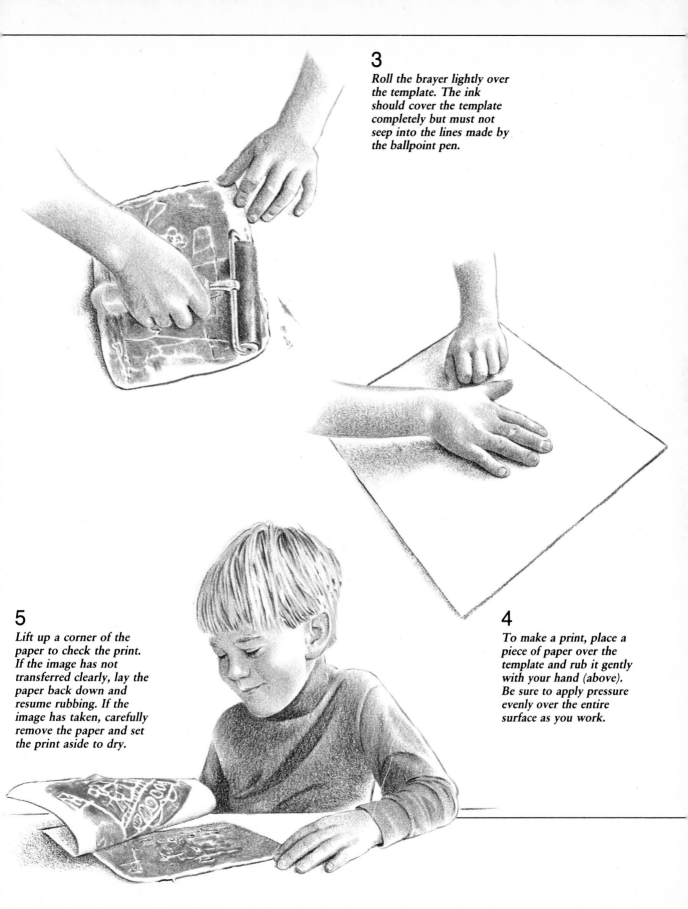

3

Roll the brayer lightly over the template. The ink should cover the template completely but must not seep into the lines made by the ballpoint pen.

4

To make a print, place a piece of paper over the template and rub it gently with your hand (above). Be sure to apply pressure evenly over the entire surface as you work.

5

Lift up a corner of the paper to check the print. If the image has not transferred clearly, lay the paper back down and resume rubbing. If the image has taken, carefully remove the paper and set the print aside to dry.

Dip-and-Dye
Paper Towels

Ages 5 to 6
Adult participation required

Materials
white paper towels or napkins
food coloring
shallow bowls
water

1
Accordion-pleat a paper towel or napkin along its entire length. The narrower the pleat, the more intricate will be the final design.

2a
For the design at top left, fold a corner of the pleated paper over to the long side, forming a triangle. Then turn the paper over and make another triangle fold (above). Alternate folds along the paper's length until you have a single triangle.

2b
The design at top right is made by folding the pleated paper in half, then halving each end to form an M (above). Try other folds to produce a variety of designs.

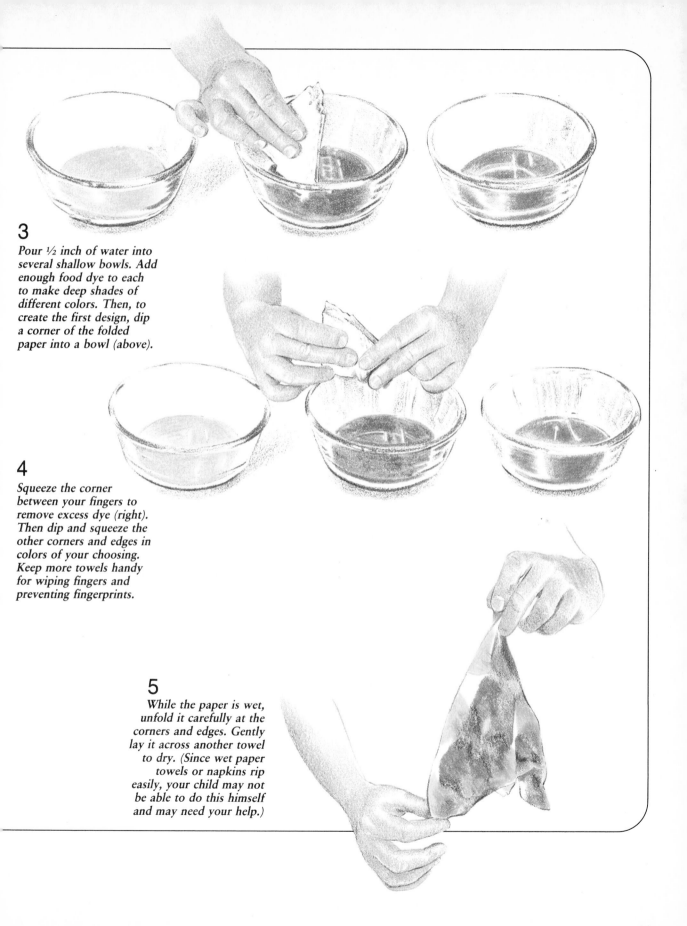

3

Pour ½ inch of water into several shallow bowls. Add enough food dye to each to make deep shades of different colors. Then, to create the first design, dip a corner of the folded paper into a bowl (above).

4

Squeeze the corner between your fingers to remove excess dye (right). Then dip and squeeze the other corners and edges in colors of your choosing. Keep more towels handy for wiping fingers and preventing fingerprints.

5

While the paper is wet, unfold it carefully at the corners and edges. Gently lay it across another towel to dry. (Since wet paper towels or napkins rip easily, your child may not be able to do this himself and may need your help.)

Found-Object Creations

There is magic in taking something ordinary, such as a paper plate or a cardboard box, and turning it into something wonderful. Transforming common objects that can be found around the house will excite your little one's imagination and will provide him with hours of hands-on learning and creative play.

Your participation. Many of the twenty-seven projects in this section are ones your youngster can complete with very little input from you. Several require an adult's skill or judgment for completion, such as when a step calls for use of a utility knife to cut corrugated cardboard. But even though you will have to perform this step yourself, you can ask your youngster to help by holding the yardstick, for instance, while you measure the cardboard. Before starting one of these more complex activities, read the instructions with an eye toward involving her along the way. She will be only too glad to help, and her participation doubtlessly will make her feel more grown-up.

Tools for Cutting Cardboard

To cut cardboard, use a utility knife *(below)*, a coping saw, or a serrated kitchen knife. A utility knife is a versatile, inexpensive tool containing a reversible blade anchored inside a handle. Utility knives and blades are available in hardware stores. A coping saw, used for cutting intricate patterns in wood or metal, has a thin, serrated blade and a metal frame.

These tools should be wielded only by an adult. When you are using a utility knife, be sure to protect your work surface with several thicknesses of newspaper or an extra piece of cardboard placed under the piece you are cutting.

By pressing the knob on the handle of a utility knife, you can bring the blade forward to cut and retract it when you are finished.

Finding the spot and the time. If you have no workroom, your kitchen is an easy-to-clean place for the more elaborate projects, since most kitchens have several large, indestructible work surfaces, as well as the convenience of running water and a sink.

When the weather is warm, you and your child might prefer to work outside, where space and cleanup present fewer problems.

Make sure that you allow enough time to complete a project, and explain to your little one before starting a complex activity with spread-out steps that it will take several days. So warned, he will not expect immediate results. Depending on his age, he may work for a couple of hours—or he may be ready to move on after only a few minutes. Allow him to take frequent breaks, and keep crayons and other materials handy for those times when you must complete a step without his help.

Plates, bags, cardboard, and boxes. The only limiting factor when it comes to found objects is your child's imagination. Inexpensive paper plates, for example, can be used to make masks such as those on pages 60-63 or puppets such as the one on page 79. Even the humble brown paper bag can be a source of fun, the basis of, among other things, charming costumes (pages 55-57) and a puppet that your child can use to act out his own scenarios.

Ordinary corrugated cardboard lends itself to dozens of uses. Light and durable, it is often available in many sizes and shapes from lamp shops, florists, moving companies, liquor stores, and supermarkets.

Major appliance boxes can be transformed into child-size clubhouses. Often you have only to cut a doorway and a window in their sides in order to create fantasy structures out of such boxes.

Use interior latex paint to cover a big project involving corrugated cardboard, such as a child-size kitchen or castle. This kind of paint adheres to the cardboard better than tempera, which can crack and peel after several days. Be prepared to use a large quantity of latex paint, since cardboard is highly absorbent.

Unlike oil-based paint, latex paint washes off with water. Your youngster, suitably dressed, should be able to use it with impunity on cardboard. Remember, though, to spread newspapers or dropcloths beneath the object to be painted. While the paint is being applied or drying, the room should be well ventilated.

Choo-Choo Costume

Ages 4 to 6

Must be made by an adult

Materials

cardboard box (about 12 x 14 x 24 inches)
utility knife
heavy-duty scissors
cardboard piece (about 14 inches square)
1½-inch-wide fabric ribbon (2 yards)
glue
interior latex enamel paint
liquid tempera paint
brushes

1

Outline and cut out an oval hole big enough for your child to step into in a sealed box's top (below), leaving about 1½ inches of cardboard on each long side. Do not remove the box's bottom flaps.

2

Starting at a narrow end of the box top, cut two slits 8 inches apart, 3 inches from what will become the costume's front edge. Cut two others about 3 inches forward from the opposite edge, 2 inches apart. The slits will be used for ribbon suspenders.

3

For handholds, cut 4-inch-wide slits in the long sides of the box, about 6 inches down from the top and 7 inches from the front edge. At each slit, cut ½ inch toward the body hole and fold the flaps in to cushion fingers (right).

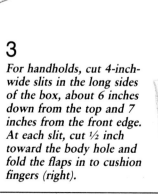

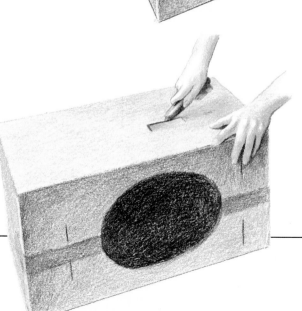

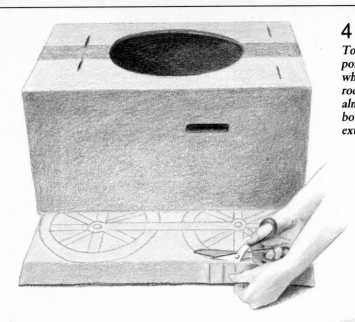

4

To make the lower portions of the large wheels and a connecting rod, draw semicircles that almost fill each side bottom flap. Cut away the extra cardboard (left).

5

On the front bottom flap, outline and cut out the cow catcher and grillwork (right). Remove the corresponding back flap. Paint the locomotive with the enamel, then apply details with the tempera.

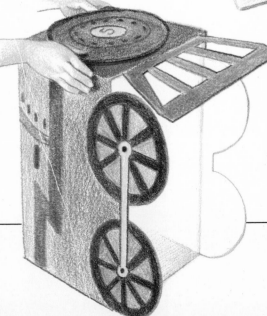

6

From the square of cardboard, fashion the circular front, making its diameter the width of the box. Paint the circle with the enamel and add details in tempera. Glue the disk to the front (left).

7

Have your child step into the box and support it at a comfortable height (right) as you insert the suspenders (below). Or you may thread them beforehand and adjust them.

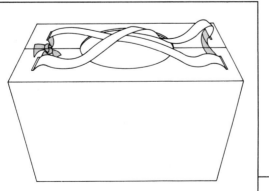

Threading suspenders. *The knotted ribbon is threaded from inside the box out through the left rear slit, in through the right front, and out through the left front. Then the ribbon is inserted into the right rear slit and tied to its other end.*

Knight Costume

Ages 4 to 6

Must be made by an adult

Materials

two sheets of posterboard
scissors
aluminum foil
silver duct tape
glue
yarn
tape measure
utility knife
two-pronged paper fasteners

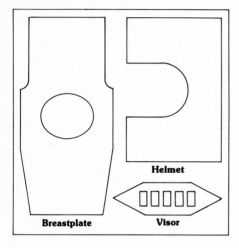

Helmet

Breastplate · Visor

Breastplate

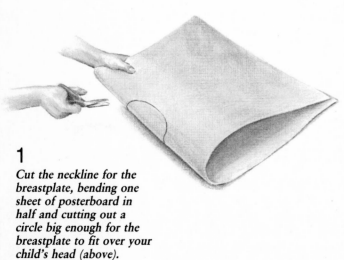

1

Cut the neckline for the breastplate, bending one sheet of posterboard in half and cutting out a circle big enough for the breastplate to fit over your child's head (above).

2

Slip the posterboard over your child's head. Mark both the back and front where his shoulders and waist end (below).

3

To trim the breastplate,
remove the posterboard
and make straight cuts
through the front and the
back from the waist to
the shoulders (below).

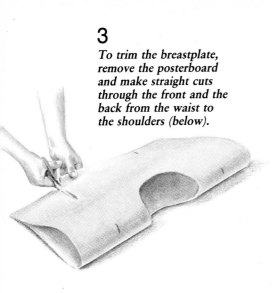

4

Refit the breastplate on
your youngster, drawing a
slightly curved line on each
side from his shoulder to
his waist (left). Remove the
posterboard and trim it
so that his arms can swing
freely. Check the fit, then
recut if necessary.

5

Apply glue to one surface
of the posterboard and
smooth foil over it. Turn it
over, fold the edges of the
foil to this side, and glue
them down. Cut out the
neck hole, leaving a 1-inch
rim. Slit the rim at
intervals and glue the tabs
to the reverse side.

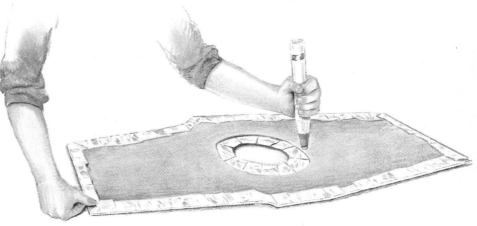

6

Tape yarn along the front
and back bottom edges
of the breastplate, making
sure it is long enough
for your child to tie the
breastplate on (left).

Helmet

1

To determine the helmet size, measure the circumference of your child's head (right).

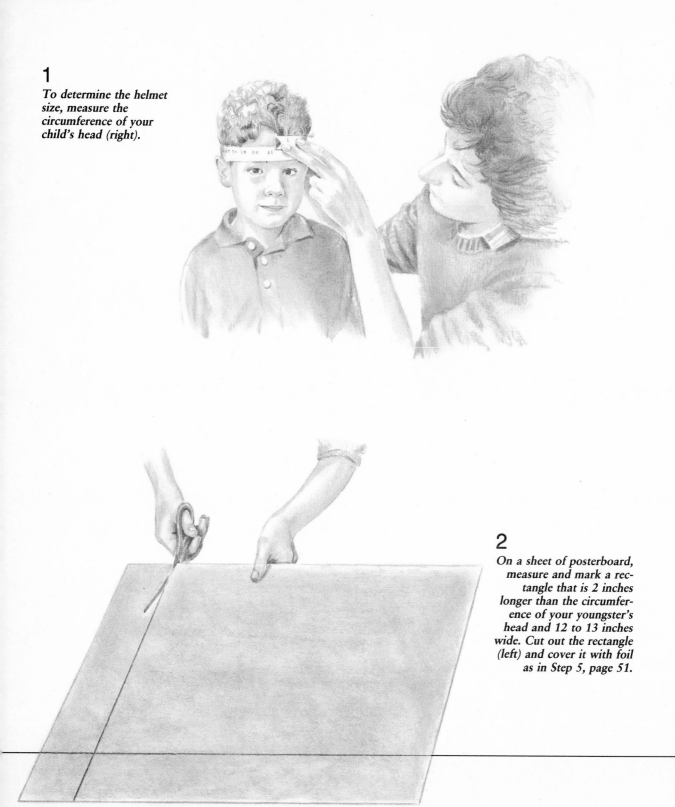

2

On a sheet of posterboard, measure and mark a rectangle that is 2 inches longer than the circumference of your youngster's head and 12 to 13 inches wide. Cut out the rectangle (left) and cover it with foil as in Step 5, page 51.

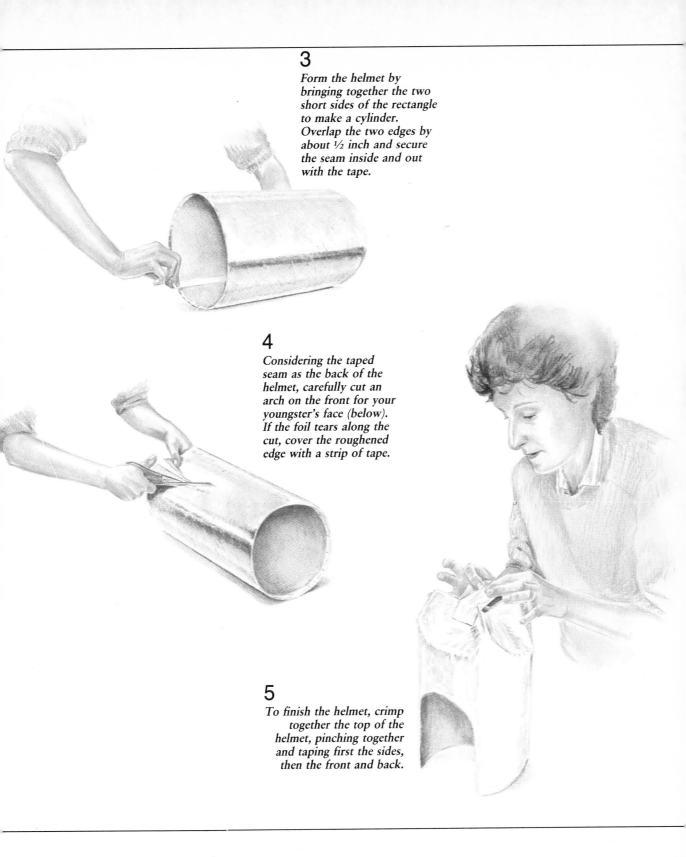

3

Form the helmet by bringing together the two short sides of the rectangle to make a cylinder. Overlap the two edges by about ½ inch and secure the seam inside and out with the tape.

4

Considering the taped seam as the back of the helmet, carefully cut an arch on the front for your youngster's face (below). If the foil tears along the cut, cover the roughened edge with a strip of tape.

5

To finish the helmet, crimp together the top of the helmet, pinching together and taping first the sides, then the front and back.

Visor

1

For a posterboard visor, cut out a rectangle 2 inches wider than the face opening and 4 to 6 inches high. Mark a center point at each end of the rectangle and trim to form angled joints. Apply glue to one surface of the visor and cover it with foil.

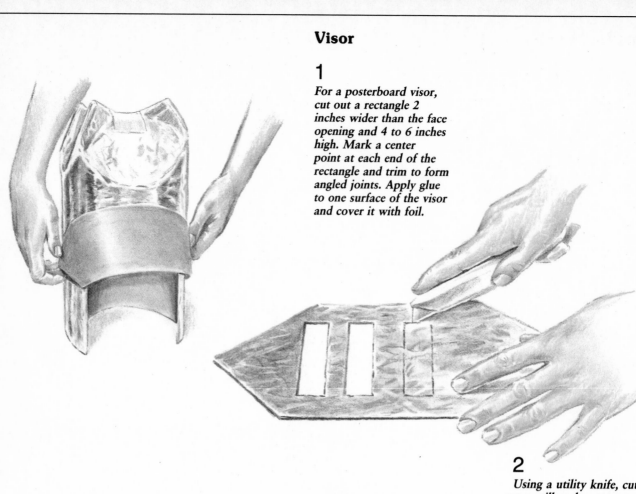

2

Using a utility knife, cut out a grillwork pattern on the visor (above). Make each opening about an inch wide to ensure that your child will have a good field of vision.

3

With the visor raised, determine where the two fasteners should go (left). Press them through the visor into the helmet. Spread apart the prongs, and tape them so that they will not scratch your child's face.

Indian Vest

Ages 4 to 6

Adult participation required

Materials

two brown grocery bags
safety scissors
tempera paints or crayons
colored construction paper
transparent tape

1

To construct the vest, turn a grocery bag upside down. Beginning at the bottom, cut a line up the center and then clip out a V-shaped neckline. Cut out an armhole on each side (above, right).

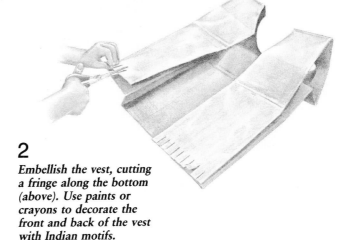

2

Embellish the vest, cutting a fringe along the bottom (above). Use paints or crayons to decorate the front and back of the vest with Indian motifs.

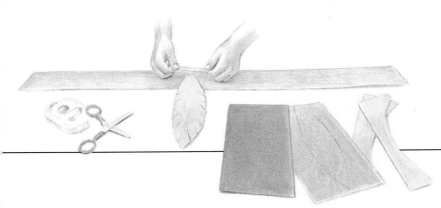

3

From a second grocery bag, cut a band that will wrap comfortably around the head. Make and fringe colored construction-paper feathers and tape them inside the band (left). Decorate the band and tape its edges.

Paper-Bag Bumblebee

Ages 4 to 6

Adult participation required

Materials

paper grocery bag
scissors
crayons or liquid tempera paint
black construction paper
two pipe cleaners
masking tape
1 yard bubble wrap

1

From the bottom of a brown grocery bag, cut out a hole large enough to fit comfortably over the head. Cut out generous armholes on each side of the bag (above).

2

Using crayons or tempera paint, decorate the front of the bag with bold black and yellow horizontal bumblebee stripes.

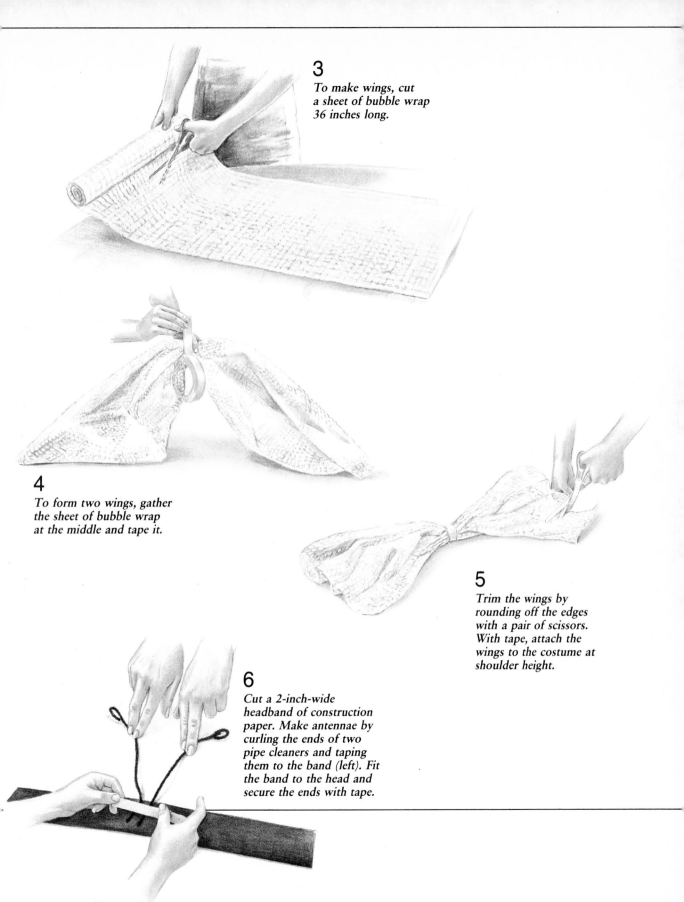

3
To make wings, cut
a sheet of bubble wrap
36 inches long.

4
To form two wings, gather
the sheet of bubble wrap
at the middle and tape it.

5
Trim the wings by
rounding off the edges
with a pair of scissors.
With tape, attach the
wings to the costume at
shoulder height.

6
Cut a 2-inch-wide
headband of construction
paper. Make antennae by
curling the ends of two
pipe cleaners and taping
them to the band (left). Fit
the band to the head and
secure the ends with tape.

Easy Paper Hats

Ages 4 to 6

Adult participation required

Made from construction paper, poster-board, and crepe paper, these hats are perfect props for imaginative play.

Police officer's cap. *Cut the basic shape for the hat from a sheet of blue construction paper. Over that, glue a visor of black construction paper and a yellow construction-paper badge. Attach the cap to a headband of construction paper or sturdier posterboard.*

Firefighter's helmet. *For durability, make this helmet from a single sheet of red posterboard. Cut out the basic helmet shape, providing a place for the head by removing the area shown in gray. Glue on a construction-paper badge matching the size of the front of the helmet as shown; finally, bend the front of the helmet forward.*

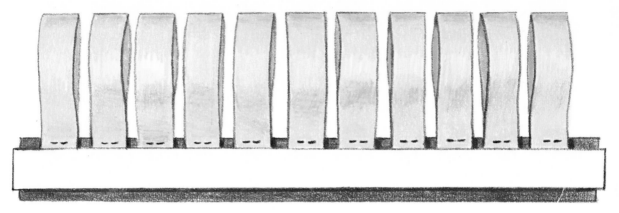

Crown. *Cut a sheet of construction paper into 1-inch-wide strips. Bend the strips in half and staple the ends to a construction-paper headband. For reinforcement, cut a second band from posterboard and glue it to the inside of the headband, covering the staples. Decorate the outside of the headband and tape the ends together.*

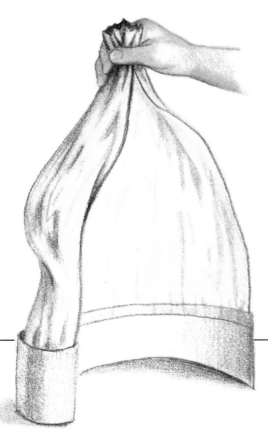

Chef's hat. *Cut a 3-inch-wide headband from white posterboard. To the inside of the band, glue a square sheet of crepe paper matching the headband's length. Gather the top edges of the crepe-paper sheet in one hand (left), and with the other bring the ends of the headband together. Tuck the gathered crepe paper inside the band and staple securely together (below).*

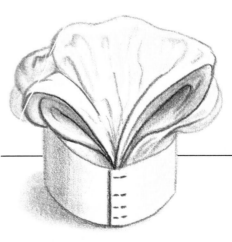

59

Foil Impressions

Ages 4 to 6

Must be made by an adult

Using aluminum foil, you can make a lifelike impression of your youngster's face that he can then decorate and hang in his room.

Materials

aluminum foil
manicure scissors
permanent markers
ribbon or yarn (optional)

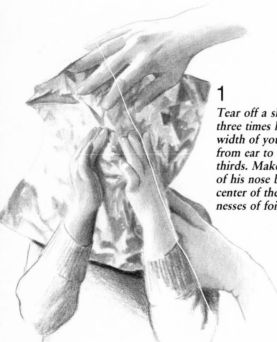

1

Tear off a sheet of foil three times longer than the width of your child's face from ear to ear. Fold in thirds. Make an impression of his nose by pressing the center of the three thicknesses of foil around it.

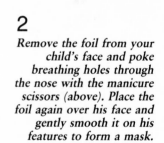

2

Remove the foil from your child's face and poke breathing holes through the nose with the manicure scissors (above). Place the foil again over his face and gently smooth it on his features to form a mask.

3

Trim excess foil from the edges of the mask. Cut generous openings for the eyes and mouth (right).

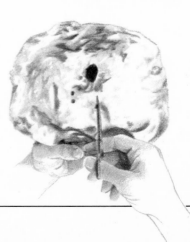

4

Decorate the mask with permanent markers (left). Poke two holes in the sides at eye level and attach a ribbon so the mask can be hung.

Masks with Handles

Ages 3 to 6

Adult participation required

Many preschoolers dislike wearing masks that cling to their faces. These are mounted on tongue depressors, which serve as handles and put the masks under the wearers' control.

Materials

paper plates
pencil
tongue depressors
heavy-duty scissors
masking tape
crayons or paint
yarn or crepe paper
cotton pompoms

Lion. *Scissor a mane around the plate edges. Draw a lion face and cut eye holes and ear slits. From a second plate, cut out ears with tabs. Insert the tabs and tape them to the back. Tape a tongue depressor to the back.*

Little girl. *Draw a face on the back of a paper plate. Cut out eyes. Roll pigtails from a length of crepe paper and tape them on. Make a horizontal slit below the mouth, insert a tongue depressor, and tape it to the front of the plate.*

Butterfly. *Outline a butterfly on the front of the plate. Cut out eyes and the shaded areas. Color the wings. Glue a pompom to the end of each attenna. Tape a tongue depressor to the back of the plate.*

Creature Faces

Ages 4 to 6

Adult participation required

Made from paper plates as on pages 60-61, these masks are attached to the head with elasticized thread.

Materials

paper plates
pencil
heavy-duty scissors
construction paper
transparent tape
liquid tempera paint
elasticized thread

Monster face. *On a plate paint a scary face with large, pointed teeth, following the shape at right. Cut away the shaded areas. Fold the rectangular part of the mask up just below the eye holes to form a snout. Bend the teeth down. Stretch a piece of elasticized thread around your head and snip it to length. Make holes at eye level on either side of the mask. Insert one end of the thread through each hole, and knot each end.*

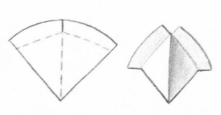

Chick. *From a plate cut out eyes and a diamond-shaped opening with sides 2¼ inches long (above left). From a second plate, draw and cut out a lower and upper beak, each a quarter circle measuring about 2¾ inches on its straight side. Fold the rounded edge of each in half; cut a slit in the center of the crease to form two tabs (above, center). Bend the tabs forward, insert them into the diamond, and tape them to the back of the plate (above, right). Paint the mask and, if you want, insert a pipe-cleaner worm in the beak.*

62

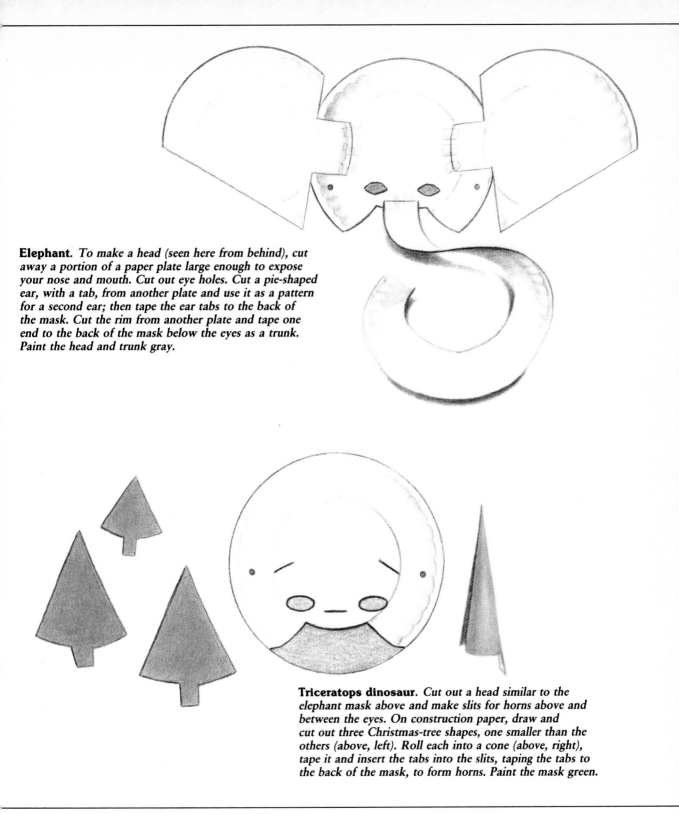

Elephant. *To make a head (seen here from behind), cut away a portion of a paper plate large enough to expose your nose and mouth. Cut out eye holes. Cut a pie-shaped ear, with a tab, from another plate and use it as a pattern for a second ear; then tape the ear tabs to the back of the mask. Cut the rim from another plate and tape one end to the back of the mask below the eyes as a trunk. Paint the head and trunk gray.*

Triceratops dinosaur. *Cut out a head similar to the elephant mask above and make slits for horns above and between the eyes. On construction paper, draw and cut out three Christmas-tree shapes, one smaller than the others (above, left). Roll each into a cone (above, right), tape it and insert the tabs into the slits, taping the tabs to the back of the mask, to form horns. Paint the mask green.*

63

Play Kitchen

Ages 4 to 6
Adult participation required

Materials

four large corrugated cardboard boxes,
  taped shut
heavy-duty fabric tape
utility knife
posterboard
aluminum foil
several sheets of corrugated cardboard
two shoe boxes: one large, one small
awl or other pointed instrument
pronged paper fasteners
interior latex and tempera paints

For the refrigerator, use a large box as storage
compartment, a smaller one as freezer. Mark doors with
a pencil. Cut along the pencil lines, leaving one side of
each door attached. Cut two strips of posterboard and
wrap them with foil. Tape a strip to each door as a
handle. Measure and cut shelves from cardboard. Tape
them in place inside the boxes; then tape the boxes
together and paint them.

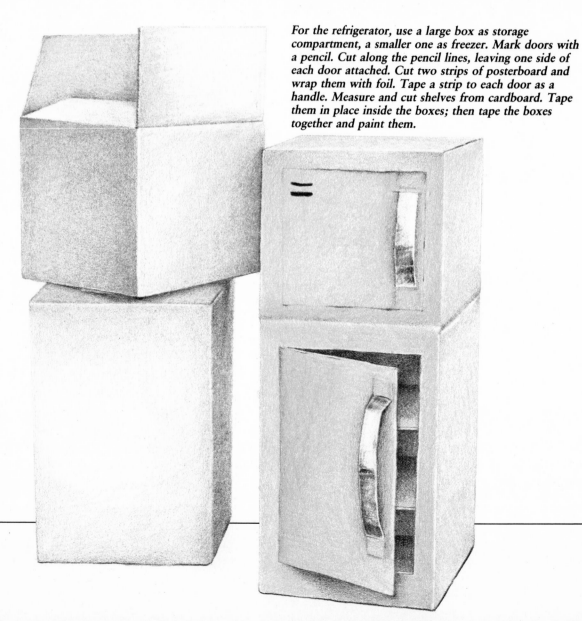

For the sink, center the large shoe box on the top of the box that will be the cabinet, and outline it. Cut out the marked area and fit the shoe box into the hole, taping it in place. Make a faucet from foil-covered posterboard and fasten it to the sink with tape. Paint the sink white and the cabinet any color you like; add details such as doors, handles, and hinges. To make the toaster, cut slots in the small shoe box and wrap the box in foil; then slit through the foil to open the slots.

Paint the box for the stove any color you like, providing details such as burners and an oven door. Make a handle out of posterboard and foil, and tape it in place. Paint a piece of cardboard and draw a clockface; tape the piece to the back of the stove. To make burner knobs that turn, cut out eight small cardboard circles, glue them together in pairs, punch holes in them and the stove with the awl, and attach them with the pronged fasteners.

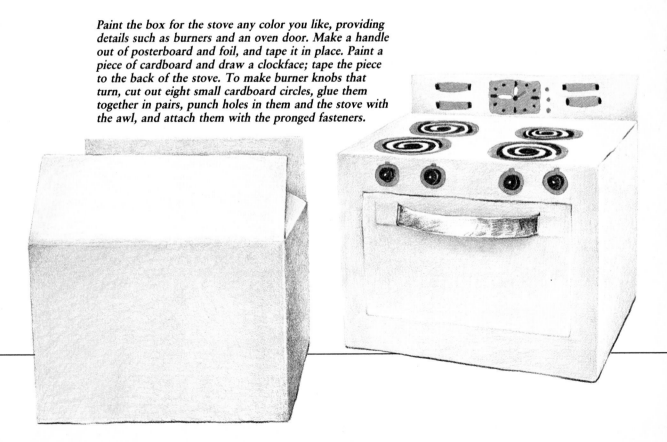

Cardboard Castle

Ages 4 to 6
Adult participation required

Gift shops, art galleries, florists, and moving companies are good sources for the boxes this project requires. The dimensions can deviate from those listed.

Materials
cardboard box (18 x 15 x 18 inches) for castle
four 3¼-inch mailing tubes for towers
eight ½-gallon milk or juice cartons for castle-tower parapets and outer-wall towers
cardboard box (19 x 6 x 6 inches) for entry tower
large, shallow box (19 x 42 x 6 inches) with detached top for outer walls
serrated kitchen knife or coping saw
pencil
heavy-duty scissors
interior latex paint

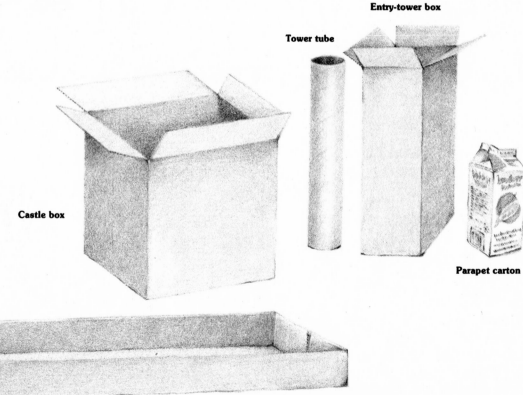

Castle box

Tower tube

Entry-tower box

Parapet carton

Outer-wall box (lid is identical)

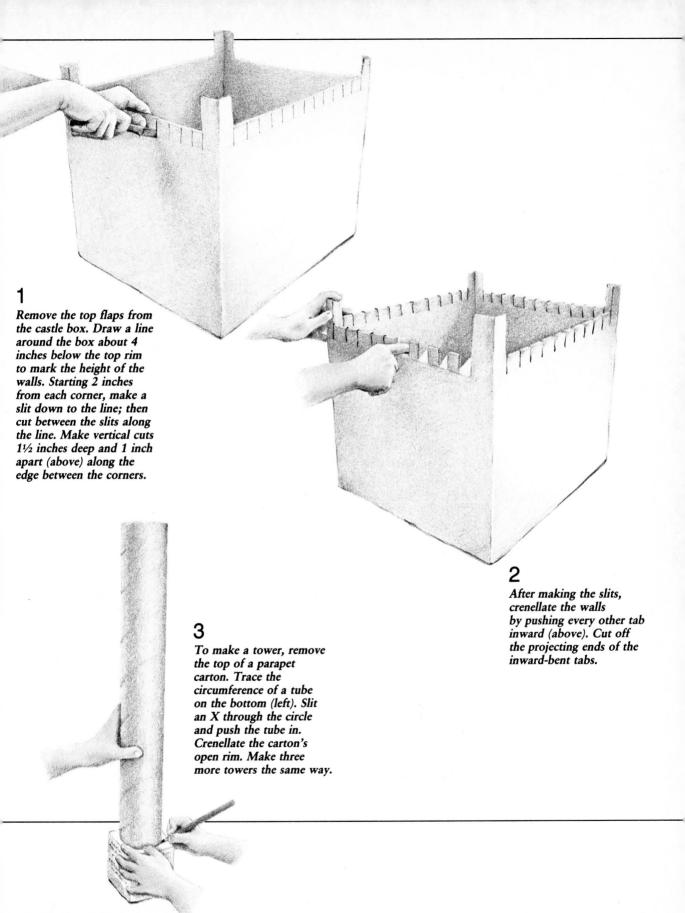

1

Remove the top flaps from the castle box. Draw a line around the box about 4 inches below the top rim to mark the height of the walls. Starting 2 inches from each corner, make a slit down to the line; then cut between the slits along the line. Make vertical cuts 1½ inches deep and 1 inch apart (above) along the edge between the corners.

2

After making the slits, crenellate the walls by pushing every other tab inward (above). Cut off the projecting ends of the inward-bent tabs.

3

To make a tower, remove the top of a parapet carton. Trace the circumference of a tube on the bottom (left). Slit an X through the circle and push the tube in. Crenellate the carton's open rim. Make three more towers the same way.

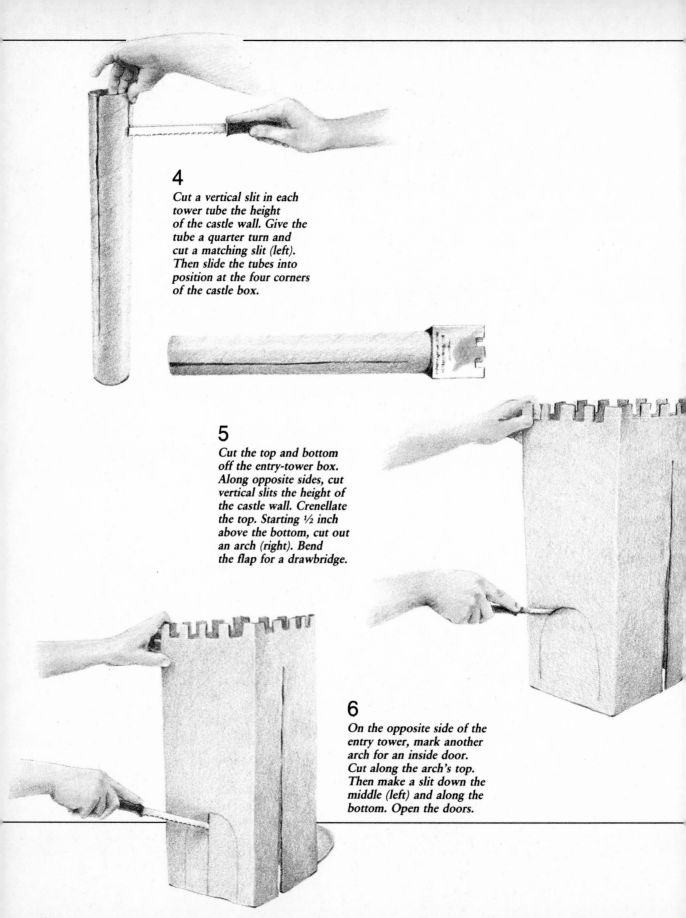

4

Cut a vertical slit in each
tower tube the height
of the castle wall. Give the
tube a quarter turn and
cut a matching slit (left).
Then slide the tubes into
position at the four corners
of the castle box.

5

Cut the top and bottom
off the entry-tower box.
Along opposite sides, cut
vertical slits the height of
the castle wall. Crenellate
the top. Starting ½ inch
above the bottom, cut out
an arch (right). Bend
the flap for a drawbridge.

6

On the opposite side of the
entry tower, mark another
arch for an inside door.
Cut along the arch's top.
Then make a slit down the
middle (left) and along the
bottom. Open the doors.

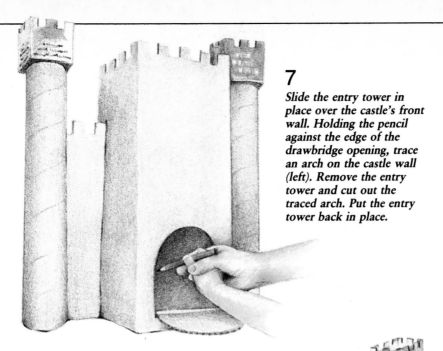

7

Slide the entry tower in place over the castle's front wall. Holding the pencil against the edge of the drawbridge opening, trace an arch on the castle wall (left). Remove the entry tower and cut out the traced arch. Put the entry tower back in place.

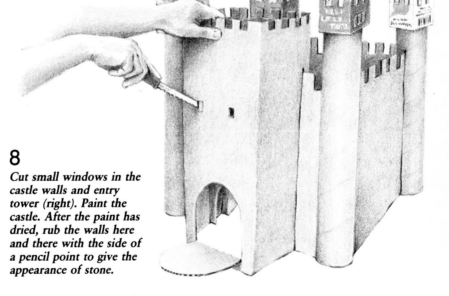

8

Cut small windows in the castle walls and entry tower (right). Paint the castle. After the paint has dried, rub the walls here and there with the side of a pencil point to give the appearance of stone.

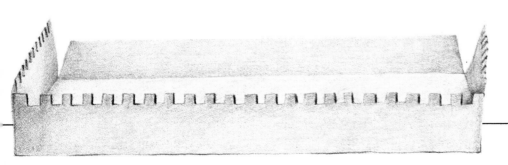

9

Crenellate three sides of the outer-wall box and its lid. Slit the corners of the remaining sides; flatten them. Overlap and tape them to make one box. Cut the tops and bottoms from four cartons for towers. Crenellate and slit the cartons, and then slide them onto the corners of the walls. Paint.

Cardboard Dollhouse

Ages 4 to 6

Adult participation required

This dollhouse is made from a single cardboard box. Furniture instructions are on pages 74-75.

Materials

large corrugated cardboard box
heavy-duty tape
ruler
pencil
spoon
utility knife
interior latex paint

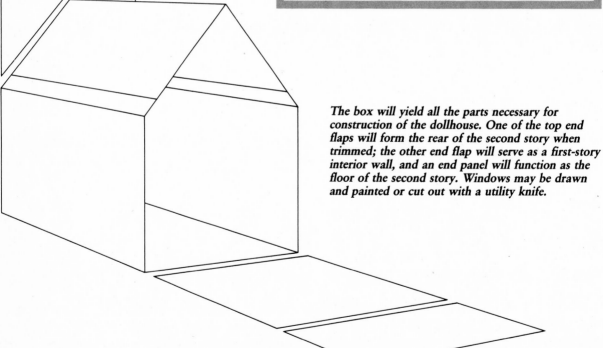

The box will yield all the parts necessary for construction of the dollhouse. One of the top end flaps will form the rear of the second story when trimmed; the other end flap will serve as a first-story interior wall, and an end panel will function as the floor of the second story. Windows may be drawn and painted or cut out with a utility knife.

1

Turn the box upside down. Reinforce the bottom edges and seams with heavy-duty tape.

2

Stand the box upright. Measure and draw a vertical line 2 inches long down each corner (below). Using a utility knife, cut each marked line. The cuts will allow you to make the peaked roof.

3

Turn the box on its side. Working on the interior surface of one side panel, draw a line connecting the bottom ends of the cuts. Press the edge of a spoon along the line, scoring a fold-line (left). Repeat on the opposite side panel.

4

Stand the box upright. Hold one of the scored side flaps in a vertical position and tape the original fold line on both sides to stiffen it (below). Repeat this process on the other side. Fold the side flaps inward along the lines scored in Step 3.

5

Bring the side flaps together to form a roof and press an end flap against them, marking where it meets the roof. Fold back the side flaps and trim the flap along the marks. Tape the roof flaps together and tape the end flap to them, completing the rear wall.

6

Cut away the remaining flap and end panel (left). Separate them, saving the panel to use as the floor for the second story and the flap for the ground-floor dividing wall.

7

To install the dividing wall for the first floor, hold the cut-off end flap upright and center it in the dollhouse. Tape the flap securely to the bottom and the rear wall of the box.

8

Slide the cut-off front panel into the box so that it rests on the dividing wall, forming a floor. Tape the panel to the box along both its upper and lower surfaces and to the wall. Paint the dollhouse.

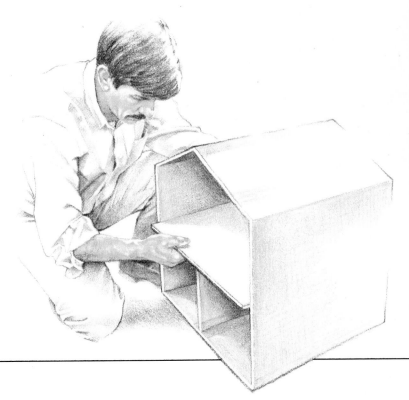

Dollhouse Furniture

Using simple tools and paint, you can improvise doll furniture from ordinary household items such as these.

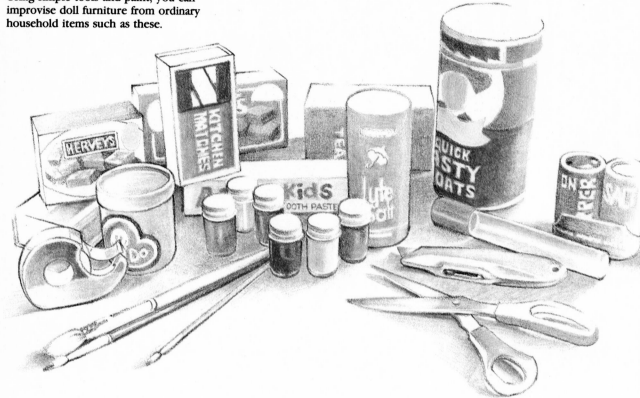

This tiny bed is made from a frozen dinner box, the headboard from a plastic-foam meat tray, and the pillow and bedspread from a rolled-up paper towel covered with fabric. The little cradle is a cardboard saltshaker with cardboard rockers taped on. A painted pill carton makes a tiny chest of drawers. A foil-covered cardboard mirror is attached to it.

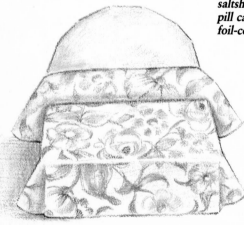

The refrigerator and range are made from kitchen
matchboxes, the sink and dishwasher from a tea box.
Cardboard is glued to the back of the range as a
panel. The kitchen table is an oatmeal box cut to size.
The stools are cardboard saltshakers cut in half, with
fabric upholstery glued on top.

The easy chair consists of two paper cups taped
together, one trimmed to form a back. The sofa's seat
is a toothpaste carton, the back a baking-chocolate
box. Both are covered with scraps of fabric. The
coffee table is fashioned from a matchbox. The floor
lamp is a pencil set in modeling dough, with a paper
cup added for a shade.

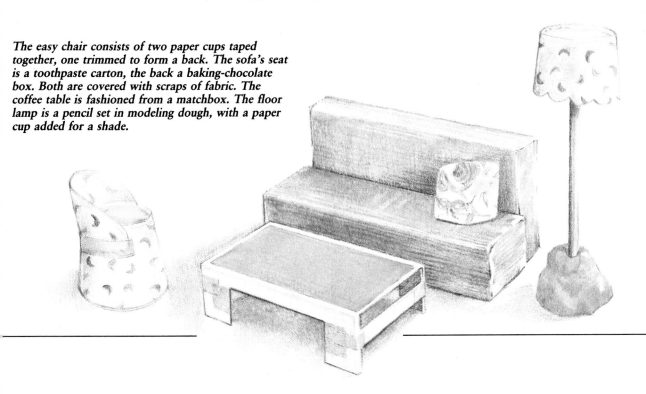

Whirly Twirly

Ages 4 to 6

The streamers are designed to flap
behind your child as he runs.

*Cut a disk from a piece of light cardboard. Poke two
holes ½ inch apart through the center. Insert the end
of a rubber band through each of the holes so that
two loops protrude on the opposite side. Pull one loop
through the other to make a single loop and tie one
end of a piece of string to it. Loop and knot the other
end for a handle. Glue crepe-paper streamers to the
back of the disk and paint a face on the front.*

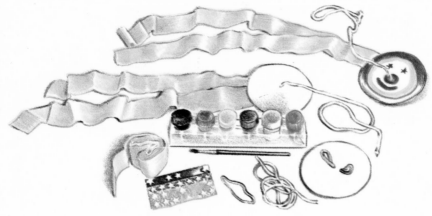

Coffee-Can Totem Pole

Ages 4 to 6

For inspiration, show your child a
picture of a totem pole.

*Cover the sides of three coffee cans with glued-on
construction paper of different colors. Use feathers,
beans, nuts, paper, dried pasta, and fabric scraps
to create different faces on each can. Top the cans
with their plastic lids and stack them as you wish.*

Egg-Carton Puppet

Ages 4 to 6

Adult participation required

To operate this puppet, put your fingers in the egg wells. The carton's top panel is a hinge for the mouth.

Materials

cardboard egg carton
heavy-duty scissors
liquid tempera paint
construction paper
glue
yarn

1

To create a mouth, open the egg carton and cut the bottom in half, extending the cut through the back of the lid (above). Turn the carton around and cut through the front side of the lid at the center. Leave the top of the lid uncut.

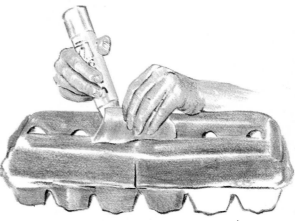

2

Spread the carton open upside down and paint it. When the paint is dry, close the lid, fitting the tabs in place. Glue the sides together to keep the lid from opening along with the mouth. Cut out a construction-paper tongue and glue it to the center of the lid (above).

3

Fold the carton in half with the tongue inside. Glue on features such as eyes, nose, and hair made from construction paper and yarn (right). Paint on lips and other details.

77

Sandwich-Bag Owl

Ages 3 to 6
Adult participation required

Materials
brown-paper sandwich bag
newspaper
cardboard toilet-paper cylinder
yarn
colored construction paper
safety scissors
glue

1
To construct the owl's head and neck, crumple a sheet of newspaper into a ball, press a toilet-paper tube into the center, and push the ball and cylinder into a sandwich bag (above). Tie yarn around the bag below the ball to secure the head (right).

3
Glue the eyes in place. To shape the ears and beak, overlap the edges of each slit by about ¼ inch and glue them to the head. Put the puppet on your child's hand, inserting his index finger into the tube. Snip holes in the front of the bag to anchor his thumb and middle finger.

2
Draw triangular wings, ears, and a beak, along with round eyes, on construction paper. Cut them out, making a ¼-inch-long slit on one side of each ear and the beak, as shown above.

Paper-Plate Frog

Ages 4 to 6
Adult participation required

Materials
paper plate
manicure scissors
colored construction paper
glue
posterboard

1

Fold a paper plate in half.
Lay it face down and on
one half partially cut out
two eyes, leaving the
portions nearest the edge
of the plate attached (left).
Fold the eyes out from the
back of the plate.

2

Cut construction paper
into two bent back legs
and two straight front legs
(below). Glue them to the
back of the plate. Make a
triangular tongue and glue
it to the front, at the fold.
Add eyeballs and lashes.

3

Cut two handles from
posterboard. Glue them
to the puppet face on
opposite sides of the fold.
Bend the puppet in half
and insert your fingers
beneath the upper handle
and your thumb beneath
the lower handle to
manipulate the frog.

Modeling Materials

No art materials are quite so tactilely appealing to youngsters as clay and its homemade variations. While pounding, patting, pulling apart, shaping, and rolling these pliable substances, your child experiences the intimacy of working with a medium that responds wonderfully to her touch and whim. In the process, she discovers different textures. She learns concepts such as thick and thin, soft and hard, wet and dry. She develops an awareness of three-dimensional design. And her control over the small muscles of her hands and fingers quickly improves as she works the clay.

The best way to introduce clay or any of these other pliable products is simply to give your youngster a fistful and let her play with it. After she has had a while to explore the material on her own, she will be ready to get the most out of the projects described in this chapter. If you want to get your child started but do not have any clay at hand, you can produce satisfactory modeling materials at home from such ingredients as flour, salt, and cornstarch. (See recipes below and soap sculpture on page 82.)

You may want to provide your youngster with a base of some sort on which to place the modeling material—a small plastic cutting board, a piece of linoleum or board, or a sheet of oilcloth or heavy vinyl. She can turn the base as she shapes her piece, and if for one reason or another she leaves the project incomplete, you can simply lift it on the base and store it on a shelf until she is ready to resume. Make sure, however, to cover it with a sheet of plastic to keep the material moist and malleable. Modeling projects can be messy, so before you allow your youngster to begin, read the tips opposite.

The following are modeling materials that you can buy for your child to use:

Natural clay: Sometimes called potter's clay, water-based natural clay is the most basic of all modeling materials and is especially responsive to handling. You can buy it in brick form at many art supply stores or hobby shops, usually in gray or terra-cotta or various shades of red. If your local dealers do not carry it, look under Ceramic Supplies or Pottery in the Yellow Pages.

A sculpture that is made of natural clay will dry when it is left exposed to the air, but since it has not been fired, it may eventually crumble. If you and your child would like to preserve her work permanently, without having to take it to a potter for firing, you might consider purchasing a self-hardening variety of clay, which contains a plastic resin that sets it firmly. After your child's sculpture has hardened, it can be covered with clear liquid shellac. Since liquid shellac is toxic, however, this step should be performed by an adult, not by a child.

Properly cared for, natural clay will last almost indefinitely. After each use, store it in a plastic bag with one or more wet sponges; their moisture will help to keep it pliable. Or scoop out a small hollow in the clay and fill it with water. Cover the bag with a second bag to ensure that the moisture will not escape, and seal both of the bags shut. Store the clay in a cool place.

A few days before your child plans to use the clay, check its condition. If it is too moist, dump it onto an absorbent surface, such as a cloth-covered board, and let it remain there for a while to dry to the proper consistency. If the clay is too hard, simply break up the larger chunks and make shallow indentations in the softer exposed portions. Fill these with water and let the clay sit overnight, tightly covered. If it is still too hard the next day, add some more water. Clay that has dried out completely calls for more drastic treatment: It has to be pulverized with a hammer and allowed to soak in water for a day or two until all of the water has been absorbed.

Modeling Materials You Can Make

Modeling Dough: In a saucepan, combine 2 cups of flour, 1 cup of salt, and 2 tablespoons of cream of tartar. Add 1 tablespoon of vegetable oil and 2 cups of water and stir over medium heat until thickened.

Cornstarch Dough: In a saucepan, combine 1 cup of cornstarch and 2 cups of baking soda. Add 3 or 4 drops of food color and 1¼ cups of cold water. Cook over medium heat for about 4 minutes, stirring constantly until it thickens to the consistency of mashed potatoes. Cover with a damp cloth so that it will not lose moisture as it cools. Knead the dough before you use it.

Salt Dough: In a bowl, combine 2 cups of flour and 1 cup of salt. Stirring, add 1 cup of water a little at a time to achieve the right consistency. Knead the dough for 10 minutes until it is smooth and supple.

A toddler merrily pulls apart a lump of modeling material, rejoicing in its texture. No special instructions are needed to get your toddler started in this delightful medium; just make sure that the clay or dough is soft and pliable so that her little fingers can manipulate it. After experimenting with it for a while, she will begin creating simple shapes and representations.

Oil-based clay substitute: Unlike natural clay, this commercial modeling material retains its pliability indefinitely. Cool temperatures, however, can stiffen it, and if kneading alone does not restore its softness, you might try incorporating a little petroleum jelly.

The product is commonly sold in boxes containing small, multicolored bricks of the material, and it comes in several consistencies. You might begin by purchasing medium-soft. Your child can decorate it using tempera to which a few drops of liquid dish detergent have been added; the detergent will help the paint to adhere.

Since this material can stain clothing, be sure to dress your little sculptor in a protective smock *(page 32)*. And since it is oil-based, your child should never put it in her mouth. For this reason, you may want to wait until she is at least three years old before giving her any to use.

Homemade modeling preparations: If you would prefer to make modeling materials instead of buying them, you can do so easily, and they will be cheaper than the store-bought products. Moreover, they are cleaner than natural clay to use and easier to manipulate. They also are appropriate for the child who is squeamish about using messy materials or who lacks sufficient finger strength to mold clay successfully. When you let your youngster help you prepare one of the recipes given opposite—for modeling dough, cornstarch dough, and salt dough—you are giving an added dimension to her play experience.

Leftover modeling dough will keep for months if it is stored in a sealed plastic bag in the refrigerator. Should it harden, all you have to do is add a few drops of water and knead it until it reaches the desired consistency. Salt dough and cornstarch dough will keep in a plastic bag in the refrigerator for about five days.

A small object fashioned from modeling dough or salt dough takes several days to air-dry. If you are in a hurry, you can bake it in a 300° F. oven for about twenty to twenty-five minutes. A larger, heavier piece requires half an hour of baking for every quarter inch of thickness. Do not bake a sculpture made of cornstarch dough; it will crack in the heat. Once dried, a piece shaped from any of these materials can be painted by your child and then, with her consent, you can give it a coating of clear liquid shellac.

Cleanup Tips

Playing with clay and other modeling materials can be messy at times. But by taking a few steps beforehand, you can avoid a time-consuming and possibly costly cleanup later.

The best place for your child to work is at a sturdy, washable table, or alternatively at the kitchen counter. Cover a more easily damaged surface, such as the dining-room table, with plastic sheeting, oilcloth, or another nonporous material. Protect the surrounding area with a plastic drop cloth or several large plastic trash bags that have been slit and attached to the floor with masking tape. Newspapers can be used in a pinch, but they can leave newsprint on a light carpet.

If your youngster has ground clay or modeling dough into the carpet with his shoes, let the particles dry, then loosen them with a stiff brush or dull knife and vacuum them up. Where oil-based clay substitute is involved, use a commercial cleaning fluid.

Soap Sculpture

Ages 3 to 6

Tell your child before he begins this activity not to rub his eyes with his fingers; they will have picked up soap.

Powdered laundry soap (not detergent) and water make a slippery—and fun to use—modeling material. To 2 cups of soap add water a tablespoon at a time, kneading until the mixture is the texture of a soft snowball. Then make a sculpture with it (right). You may also shape it into a ball and place it on a piece of cardboard to dry overnight. After the soap has hardened, you can sculpt it with a teaspoon.

Sculpting Together

Ages 4 to 6

Many older preschoolers and kindergartners find working on a clay sculpture with a friend fun.

With a playmate, pull clay apart into fist-size chunks and flatten a large piece into a base. You can then build up your piece from the base however you see fit, either working together or taking turns.

Thumb Pots

Ages 3 to 6

This is a good introduction to pottery making. But let your child get used to manipulating clay through a few hours of free play before having him start to make pots.

Materials

clay or other modeling material
  (recipes, page 80)
liquid tempera paint
narrow paintbrush

1

Using your palms, roll a fistful of clay into a small ball. Press the ball against the table to form a base. Make an indentation in the top of the ball with your thumb (below).

2

Widen the indentation by pressing the clay gently between your thumb and forefinger while turning the ball with your other hand. When the pot has been shaped, set it aside so it can dry.

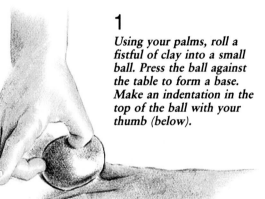

3

Decorate the dried pot with liquid tempera paint. To make intricate designs, dip the bristles of a narrow paintbrush in water and shape the wet bristles into a point with your fingers before applying the paint.

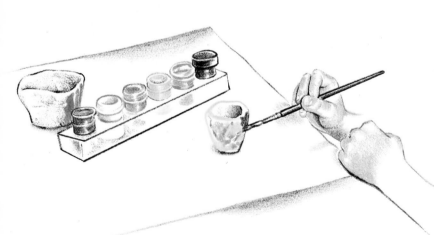

Clay Jewelry

Ages 4 to 6
Adult participation required

Materials
salt dough or cornstarch dough
  (recipes, page 80)
baby-food jar lid
wax paper
pencil
button
watercolor paints
paintbrushes
clear liquid shellac
large safety pin
heavy-duty fabric tape

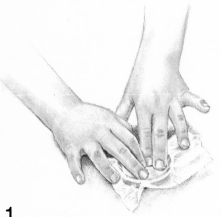

1

To make a brooch, line the lid with wax paper that extends well beyond the edges. Press some dough into the lid (above) until it is level with the rim. Smooth it with your fingers until it fits snugly.

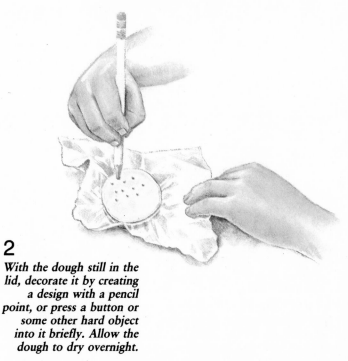

2

With the dough still in the lid, decorate it by creating a design with a pencil point, or press a button or some other hard object into it briefly. Allow the dough to dry overnight.

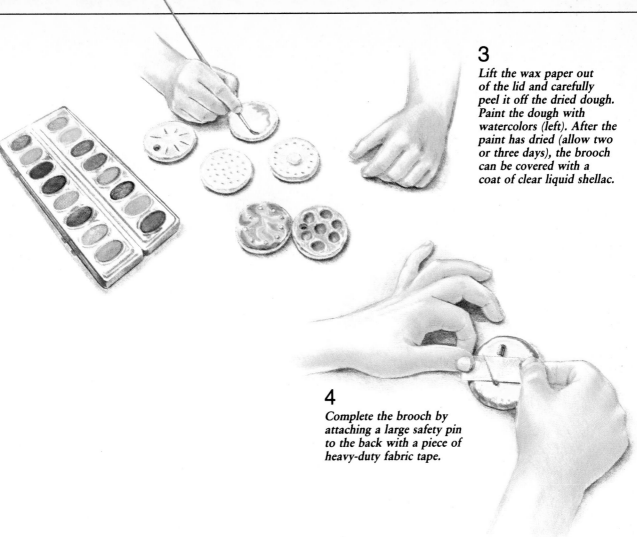

3

Lift the wax paper out of the lid and carefully peel it off the dried dough. Paint the dough with watercolors (left). After the paint has dried (allow two or three days), the brooch can be covered with a coat of clear liquid shellac.

4

Complete the brooch by attaching a large safety pin to the back with a piece of heavy-duty fabric tape.

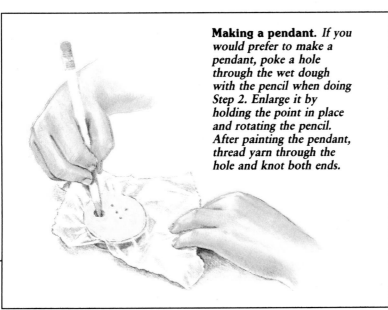

Making a pendant. *If you would prefer to make a pendant, poke a hole through the wet dough with the pencil when doing Step 2. Enlarge it by holding the point in place and rotating the pencil. After painting the pendant, thread yarn through the hole and knot both ends.*

Papier-Mâché Dragon

Ages 4 to 6

Adult participation required

With your assistance, your child can create a menagerie of creatures.

Materials

newspapers, including color comics
masking or packing tape
premixed wallpaper paste
shallow bowl
scissors
liquid tempera paint
paintbrushes

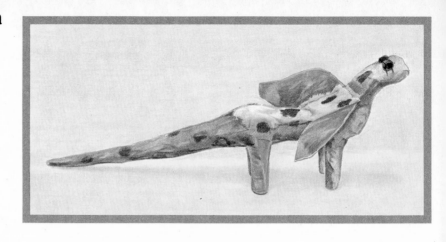

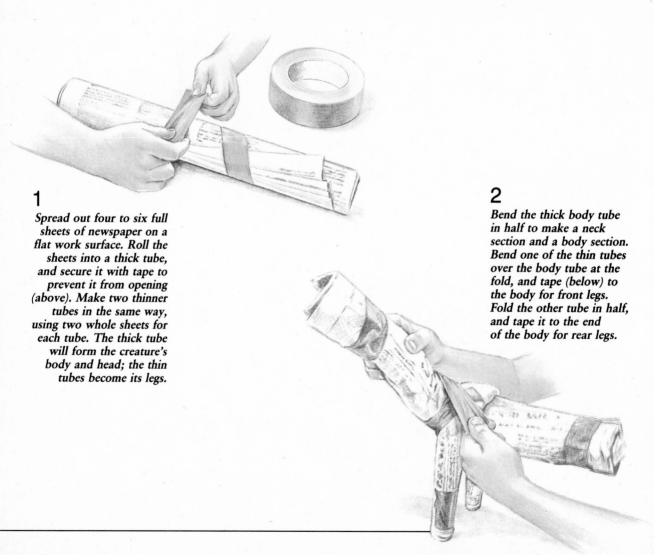

1

Spread out four to six full sheets of newspaper on a flat work surface. Roll the sheets into a thick tube, and secure it with tape to prevent it from opening (above). Make two thinner tubes in the same way, using two whole sheets for each tube. The thick tube will form the creature's body and head; the thin tubes become its legs.

2

Bend the thick body tube in half to make a neck section and a body section. Bend one of the thin tubes over the body tube at the fold, and tape (below) to the body for front legs. Fold the other tube in half, and tape it to the end of the body for rear legs.

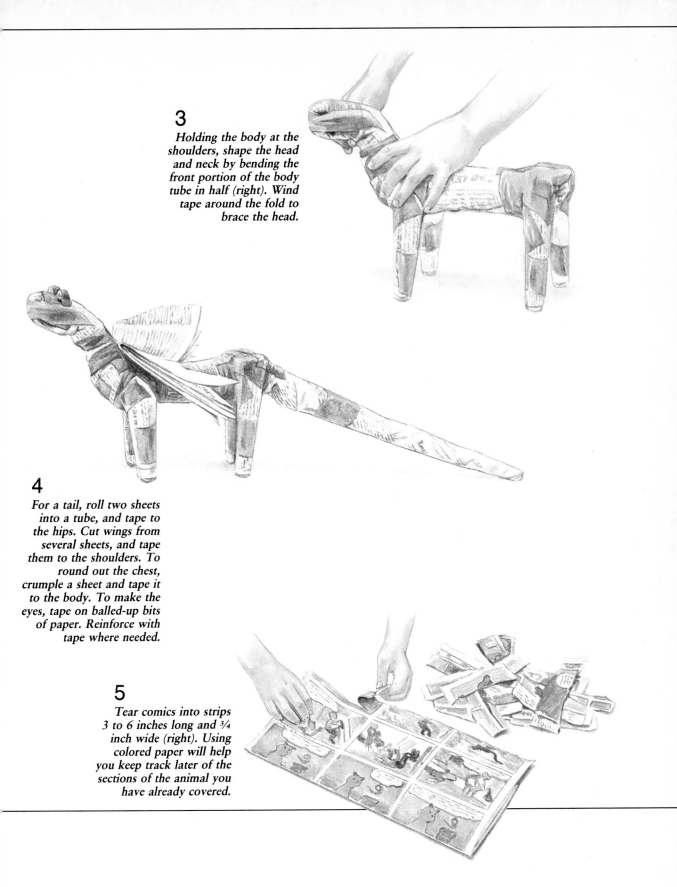

3

Holding the body at the shoulders, shape the head and neck by bending the front portion of the body tube in half (right). Wind tape around the fold to brace the head.

4

For a tail, roll two sheets into a tube, and tape to the hips. Cut wings from several sheets, and tape them to the shoulders. To round out the chest, crumple a sheet and tape it to the body. To make the eyes, tape on balled-up bits of paper. Reinforce with tape where needed.

5

Tear comics into strips 3 to 6 inches long and ¾ inch wide (right). Using colored paper will help you keep track later of the sections of the animal you have already covered.

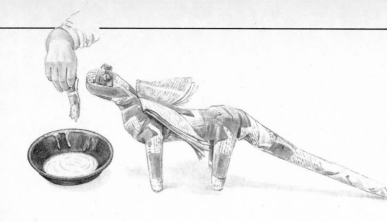

6

Pour a little wallpaper paste into a bowl. Dip a strip of the comics into the paste to coat the paper thoroughly. Let excess glue drip back into the bowl (left) before pasting the strip on the figure.

7

Beginning wherever you like, drape the strips over the figure, but be sure that they partially overlap. Smooth the excess glue over the surface as you work. Apply an extra layer or two, or as many as needed for reinforcement.

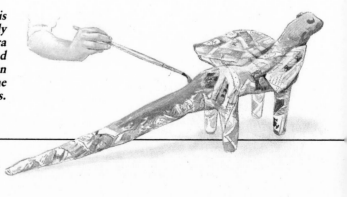

8

With cardboard supports under the wings, set the dragon in a warm, dry location to harden. After 24 hours, test for dryness. If the surface feels cool, the inside is still damp and needs more time to dry.

9

When the dragon is completely dry, apply several coats of tempera paint. Yarn hair and various decorations can be pasted on once the paint itself dries.

Papier-Mâché Bird

Ages 4 to 6
Adult participation required

This fanciful bird is made with the same materials and techniques used for the dragon *(pages 86-88)*.

1

Crumple newspaper into two balls, a larger one for the body and a smaller one for the head. Wrap tape around each ball so it will hold its shape, then tape the two together (above).

2

For the beak, fashion a small cone, about 3 inches long, out of a half sheet of newspaper and secure it with tape (right). Tape the beak to the head. Crinkle up wads of paper for eyes, and tape them on.

3

For legs, roll three sheets of newspaper together. Lay them across the body, and bend the ends up to form feet. Secure the legs with tape. Cut a tail from two layers of paper and attach it with tape (below).

4

After applying strips of papier-mâché (Steps 6 and 7, opposite), set the bird in a warm place to dry, with the belly and any other sagging sections propped up (below). Paint the bird after the paste has dried.

Working with Fabrics

Thanks to their suppleness, vibrant colors, and varied textures, fabrics are a natural for children's arts and crafts activities. Projects made from fabrics can be displayed permanently, or even in some instances worn or otherwise used —and what, from a child's point of view, could be a bigger source of pride than that?

Awakening your youngster's enthusiasm for playing with fabric will not be difficult. To help pique his interest, let him look through a magnifying glass at a piece of burlap or loosely woven cloth. Point out how each strand passes over and under other strands. Show him the loops in a swatch of knitted fabric, and let him run his fingers over the ridges in a piece of corduroy.

Incorporating fabrics into art activities. You need not look far for material to use in projects. If your ragbag fails you, see whether your local fabric or sewing shop will give you some samples. Include a fabric-scrap box among your youngster's art supplies and have some sewing tools at the ready, along with balls of yarn and lengths of ribbon.

Your child can use an assortment of scraps to produce a striking collage *(opposite)*. Or he can press bits of cloth into a flattened piece of clay to leave imprints. You might also have him place a thin sheet of paper over some textured fabric and make a rubbing with the side of a crayon. Youngsters like using yarn in their projects, laying it down on lines of white glue dribbled onto a piece of paper; all sorts of colorful designs can be built up this way.

Stitchery. Stitching has much the same appeal for young children as drawing. They can make lines or designs with yarn or thread. And the physical activity of moving a blunt-ended plastic embroidery needle up and down through the fabric appeals to a preschooler's desire to manipulate things.

Fabrics and Fibers

The fabrics, fibers, and supplies listed below are particularly suited to preschoolers' creative use.

Fabrics
burlap	nylon net
woven dishcloths	mesh onion bags
large-gauge	nylon screening
needlepoint fabric	felt

Fibers
household string	dental floss
yarn	shoelaces

Other supplies
large-holed buttons	fabric ribbon
rickrack	plastic-foam trays
ice-cream or craft	plastic embroidery
sticks	needle

Threading a shoelace through prepunched holes in a sewing card is an easy way for two- and three-year-olds to begin. You can make sewing cards at home, using pieces of light cardboard and a hole punch. A four-year-old will enjoy poking the embroidery needle threaded with yarn through a piece of plastic foam cut from a supermarket meat tray. The yarn, from knot to needle, should be no longer than your child's forearm so that he can easily work with it.

To start your older preschooler on a sewing project, place some loosely woven fabric—a dishcloth, for example, or even a mesh onion bag—in an embroidery hoop and give your youngster a yarn-threaded embroidery needle. At first his work will be haphazard and probably aimed at using up all the yarn. As he becomes more skilled, he will try to stitch designs. Avoid giving him drawn patterns to follow; he will create his own as he goes. Let him have some buttons, beads, macaroni, plastic-foam packing nuggets, or other interesting items to incorporate into his stitchery.

Weaving. To introduce your youngster to weaving's basics, make him a weaving card. With a single-edged razor blade, cut long, parallel slits in a sheet of lightweight cardboard about one-and-one-half inches apart, leaving about an inch

Concentration shows on the face of a toddler as he works a strand of heavy yarn through an unexpected loom, a chain-link fence. With help from his mother, he is managing the basic over-and-under pattern of weaving.

uncut at top and bottom. Reinforce the cardboard's edges with masking tape to prevent tearing. Show your child how to pass lengths of contrasting colored paper over and under the slits. When he makes mistakes, tell him that they only add interest to his weaving and encourage him to continue. And when he is finished, show him how to securely fasten the ends of the woven paper strands with tape.

If you prefer to introduce weaving with yarn, thread, or string instead of paper strips, you can make a basic loom from materials as common as a shoe box or a piece of stiff cardboard *(pages 92-93)*. After wrapping yarn around the loom to form the warp, have your youngster weave his yarn through the warp. Demonstrate how to pass over the first strand and under the second, reversing the pattern in the second row. However imprecise your young weaver's final results, he will have gotten the idea, and may now want to experiment with new patterns—going over two and under one, or taking a more free-form approach. As he reaches school age, he may be accomplished enough to embark on a more sophisticated weaving project, such as the Eye of God *(pages 94-95)*, which requires considerable cognitive skill and small-muscle coordination.

Dyeing fabric. Older preschoolers and kindergartners are likely to find tie-dyeing *(pages 96-97)* an absorbing activity. Tie-dyeing knows no mistakes; however uniformly or randomly the tying is done, interesting patterns always develop.

Choose nontoxic commercial dyes and mix them yourself to avoid accidents; then help your youngster with the basic folds. Accordion-folding the fabric lengthwise and then tying it off at intervals will give a linear design, while tying puckers or gathering fabric around marbles or other small objects will produce circular patterns. Knotting the fabric will yield yet another effect. You and your youngster can tie-dye pieces of fabric for display or dye cotton clothing, such as T-shirts, for you both to wear.

Cloth Collage

Ages 3 to 6

Less likely to tear than paper, fabric scraps are ideal for a collage.

Give your child a plain but colorful background piece of fabric, about typing-paper size, and let him arrange scraps of fabric, bits of ribbon, buttons, and other sewing materials on it as he likes. Show him how to stick each piece to the background with a drop or two of glue.

Cardboard Loom

Ages 4 to 6
Adult participation required

A simple cardboard loom supports a young weaver's early efforts, then forms an attractive frame for the finished piece.

Materials
6-inch square of corrugated cardboard
heavy-duty scissors
string, yarn, or dental floss
ribbon or strips of fabric

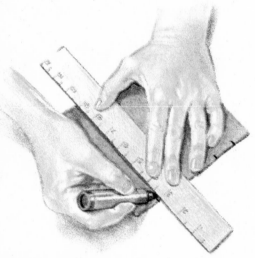

1
Starting from a corner, measure and mark 1-inch intervals along an edge of the cardboard. Repeat on the opposite edge.

2
Using a pair of heavy-duty scissors, cut a ½-inch slit at each mark on both edges of the cardboard. The slits will serve to hold the warp firmly in place.

3

Knot a 5-foot piece of string 2 inches from one end. Slip the knot into the first slit on one side of the cardboard. Then pull the string over the cardboard and through the opposite slit, across the back of the loom, and into the second slit. Now bring the string forward and down into the opposite slit, and so on, until the string has been wrapped entirely around the loom, forming the warp.

4

To complete the warp, bring the free end of the string across the back of the loom and tie it to the knotted end (right); cut off the excess. Then use a piece of the leftover string to tie a short loop onto the back of the warp; use the loop to hang the piece.

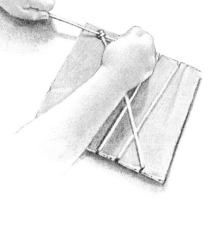

5

Weave a strip of ribbon or fabric across the warp, moving over one string and under the next (right). Add more rows, reversing the over-and-under order with each row, until the weaving is complete.

Eye of God

Ages 5 to 6
Adult participation required

Attractive from front or back, this traditional ornament can be made with one color or with multicolored yarn *(right)*. Because the first steps are intricate, begin the project for your child and help him until he is comfortable with the basic technique of the weaving.

Materials

two craft sticks or ice-cream sticks
glue
scissors
multicolored yarn

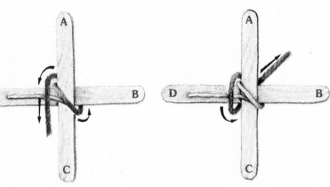

1

Glue the sticks together in a cross and dry them overnight. Anchor the yarn with your thumb on arm D (far left). Bring the yarn over the center of the cross and to the right of arm C; then wrap it twice around the cross intersection diagonally, ending up to the left of arm A (left).

2

To reverse the direction of the wrapping, bring the yarn down in front of arm D (far left). Then pull the yarn diagonally behind the cross intersection to the right of arm A (left).

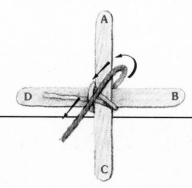

3

Beginning at the right of arm A, wrap the yarn diagonally around the intersection twice, ending in front of the sticks and to the left of arm C (left).

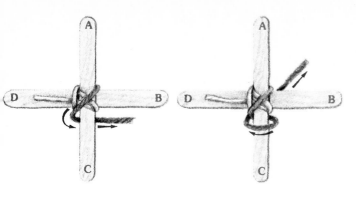

4

Wrap the yarn once around arm C by bringing the yarn behind it from left to right (far left) and around and across the front; then pull the yarn behind the intersection and to the right of arm A (left).

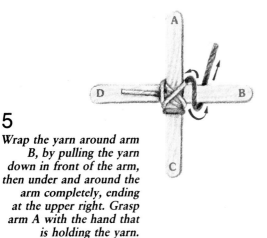

5

Wrap the yarn around arm B, by pulling the yarn down in front of the arm, then under and around the arm completely, ending at the upper right. Grasp arm A with the hand that is holding the yarn.

6

Rotate the cross a quarter turn clockwise, so that arm A is now to the right. Wrap the yarn one turn around A just as you did in Step 5; then rotate the cross another quarter turn, and wrap the yarn around the new right-hand arm. Continue wrapping and turning, until the rows are within ½ inch of the tips of the cross's arms.

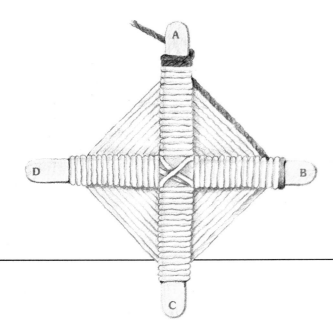

7

Glue the last ½ inch of the last arm you wrapped and then wind three more turns of the yarn around it, pressing the yarn firmly into the glue. Cut off the excess. Tie a second piece of yarn, 8 inches long, tightly around the arm, and then tie its ends together into a loop for hanging (opposite, top).

Tie-Dyeing

Ages 4 to 6
Adult participation required

Choose light-colored cotton or unbleached muslin fabric for this project. Synthetics do not dye as well.

Materials

white or light-colored fabric
rubber bands
cold-water fabric dye
rubber gloves
large enamel pot or old plastic dishpan
wooden dowel or long-handled spoon
heavy-duty scissors
clothesline

1
To make a pattern of straight lines, like the one on the left in the picture at the top of this page, first fold the entire piece of fabric back and forth in accordion pleats.

2
Bind the pleated fabric tightly with several rubber bands at intervals. At each rubber band a white stripe will be created because the tight folds will keep the dye from penetrating.

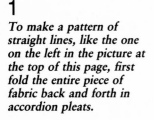

3
Prepare the dye in the pot according to package directions. Soak the fabric in the dye, stirring gently (left). Put rubber gloves on and then, with the wooden dowel or spoon, lift the fabric into the sink.

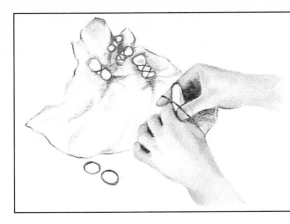

For a circle pattern.
Pull together several separate clumps of material and bind each one tightly with a rubber band (left). Dye the fabric as described in Steps 3 through 6.

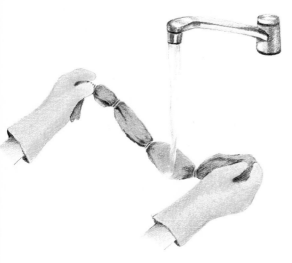

4

With the rubber bands still in place, rinse the dyed fabric, first in hot running water and then in cold, until the rinse water runs clear. Remove the fabric from the sink and lay it on a stack of newspaper.

6

Hang the fabric to dry on a clothesline (below); catch the drips with newspapers on the floor. When the fabric is dry, you may want to tie it again and dye it with a darker color. Iron out the wrinkles.

5

Using scissors, cut away the rubber bands. Be sure to hold each one as you snip it, to prevent it from flying off (below).

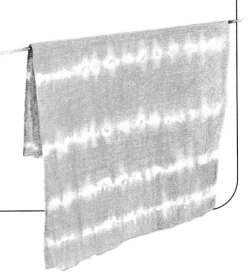

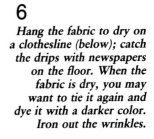

Crafts for Special Occasions

Celebrations—birthdays, holidays, and religious observances—are the stuff of childhood memories, and often the milestones by which you measure your child's development. Crafts projects can be an integral part of such happy family times. Not only are they fun in themselves; they also imbue the occasions for which they are intended with added personal meaning. What is more, they make your child a direct participant in treasured events and traditions.

Such projects are the subject of this chapter. It starts with gifts your child can make: old-fashioned silhouette drawings, plaster hand prints, and a T-shirt that is gaily decorated with fabric crayon. The act of giving a handmade present, such as the carefully wrapped puppet that the girl at right is proudly presenting to her grandmother, teaches your child that giving can indeed be just as satisfying as receiving. And for you such gifts are precious reminders of your youngster's growing skills and creativity.

Next come seasonal projects, beginning with Valentine cutouts and collages, St. Patrick's Day napkin holders, colored Easter eggs and decorations, a Passover matzo cover and Elijah cup, and Fourth of July cotton-ball fireworks and flag. Following those are a number of items to make for Halloween—paper pumpkins, crepe-paper spider webs, and a scarecrow mobile. And finally, to mark the winter holidays, there are paper turkeys for Thanksgiving, a star of David and a menorah for Hanukkah, and dough and paper decorations for Christmas.

Printed Gift-Wrap

Ages 4 to 6

You can print your own festive
wrapping paper for any occasion.

*Print your own tissue-paper gift-wrap with kitchen
sponges that are cut into holiday shapes using the
techniques shown on page 40. Spread out a doubled
sheet of tissue paper on an impermeable surface. Dip the
sponges in tempera paint, to which a few squeezes of
liquid dish detergent have been added, and press them
against the tissue. Let the tissue dry in place to avoid
ripping the damp paper.*

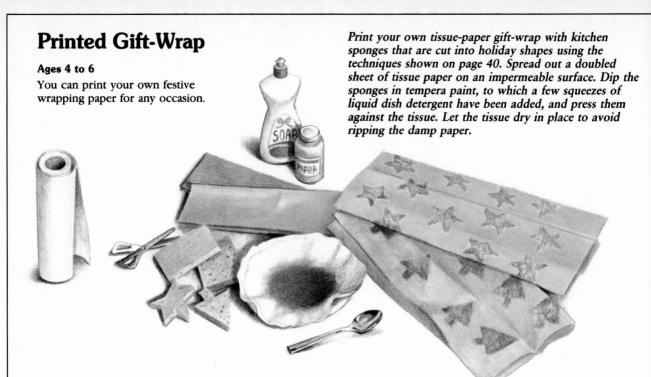

Hand-Print Plaque

Ages 4 to 6

Adult participation required

Do not pour plaster of Paris—a
quick-setting paste when mixed with
water, available at craft shops—down
the sink; it can damage plumbing.

Materials

plaster of Paris
empty coffee can
wooden dowel or other stirrer
plastic plate or disposable pie pan
awl or large nail
yarn or ribbon

1
*Pour ½ cup of water into
the coffee can and add 1
cup of plaster of Paris. Stir
with the dowel until the
mixture is the consistency
of pancake batter.*

2

Slowly pour the plaster of Paris into the plate, to a depth of about ½ inch below the edge. Do not let the plaster rise higher or it will overflow when you press your hand into it.

3

Press your hand, fingers apart, into the plaster and leave it until the plaster has set—about two minutes. To test, lift one finger gently; if the edge of the impression stays firm, remove your hand.

4

As soon as you remove your hand, use the awl to make a hole in the plaster above the finger marks for a hanger. Let the plaque dry overnight, then slip it from the plate. Or use the plate as a frame, punching the hanger hole through it and holding the plate and plaque together with the hanger yarn (opposite).

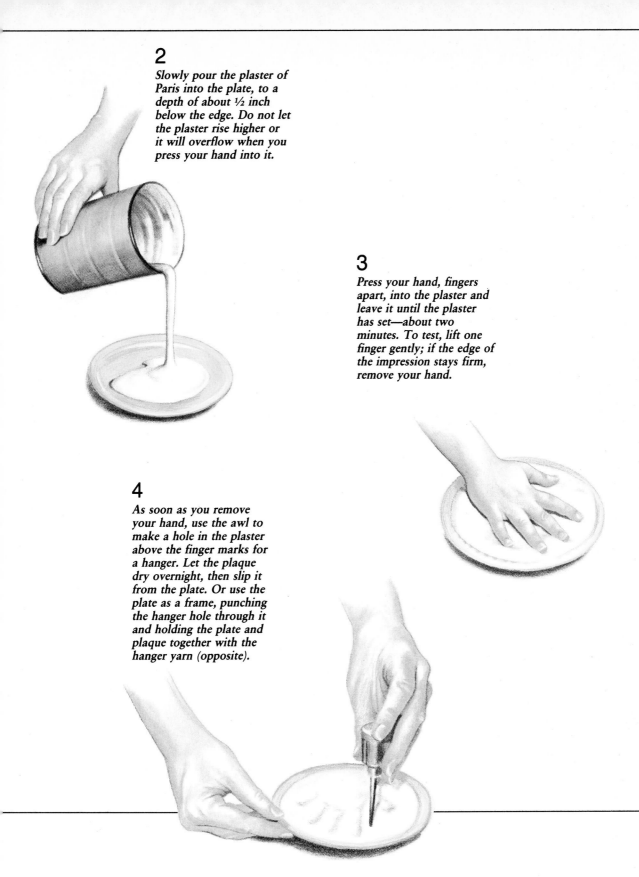

Silhouette

Ages 4 to 6

Adult participation required

Materials

one sheet each of 12-by-18-inch black and
    white construction paper
pushpins or masking tape
lamp with unshaded bulb or a slide projector
pencil
safety scissors
glue

1

*The child should sit in a
straight-backed chair
placed sideways against a
blank wall. Pin or tape a
sheet of black construction
paper to the portion of the
wall behind her head (left).*

2

*Place the unshaded lamp
about 10 feet away from
the child and adjust it until
the shadow of her profile
is crisp and centered on
the black paper.*

3

*With a pencil, outline the
shadow profile on the
paper. Work as quickly as
you can, because it will
be hard for a child to keep
still for very long.*

4

Cut out the silhouette from the paper, tilting the paper so that the pencil line glistens against the black and makes a clear guide.

5

Apply glue to the back of the silhouette (below), and center the silhouette on the white construction paper, smoothing it evenly and gently as shown in the picture above, left.

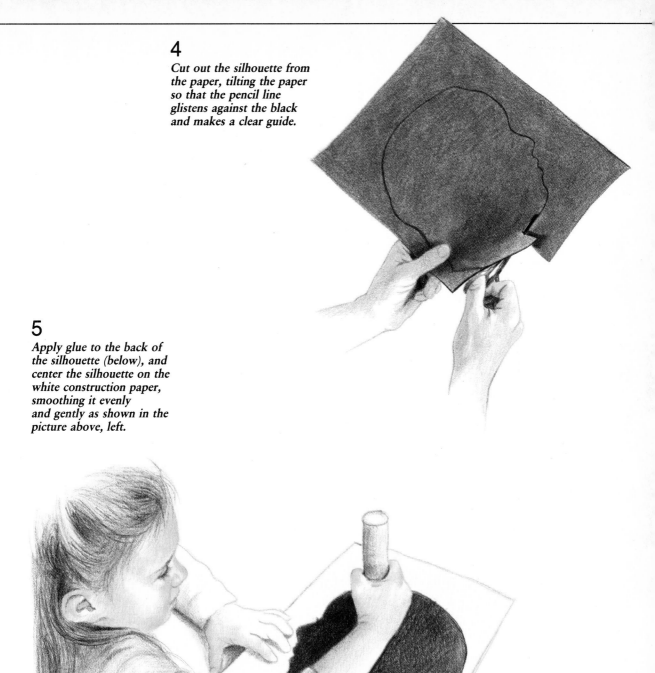

Crayon-Transfer Shirt

Ages 3 to 6

Adult participation required

Materials

T-shirt made from at least 50 percent
   synthetic fibers
transfer fabric-marking crayons
   (available in most fabric shops)
typing paper
cardboard cut to fit inside shirt
iron

1

*Using the crayons, draw a
picture on the typing
paper. Press hard on the
crayons, and fill in the
drawing so the colors will
transfer well. Lay the shirt
on an ironing board, and
slide the cardboard inside.*

2

*Place the drawing face
down on the shirt, and
cover it with a sheet of
paper. With a hot iron,
transfer the drawing to the
shirt. Let the papers cool,
then peel them away.*

Light Catcher

Ages 4 to 6
Adult participation required

Materials
tissue paper in several colors
clear plastic self-adhesive covering
safety scissors
hole punch
decorative cord or ribbon for hanger

1

Cut out a simple shape from the self-adhesive covering. Trace and cut out an identical shape. Peel the protective paper from one of these (above) and lay the shape on a table, sticky side up.

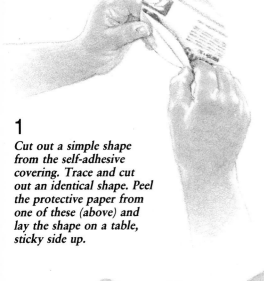

2

Using scissors, snip small pieces of tissue paper into different shapes. Arrange the snippets, overlapping some, on the adhesive surface. When the design is complete, peel the paper from the matching piece of self-adhesive covering, and lay the shape sticky side down on the design.

3

Trim the completed design to give it a neat appearance. Punch a small hole near the top, and thread an 8-inch length of cord or ribbon through it (below). Tie a bow in the cord and hang the piece.

Snowstorm Jar

Ages 4 to 6
Adult participation required

Materials
empty baby-food jar with lid
small piece of felt
pen or pencil
safety scissors
water-resistant glue
narrow fabric ribbon
plastic Christmas-tree ornament
distilled water
nonmetallic white glitter

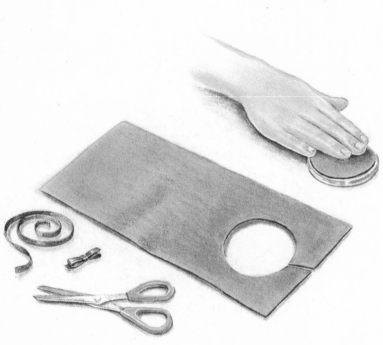

1

Outline the lid on the felt, then cut the felt to fit the lid. Glue it to the lid (left). Cut the ribbon to fit around the lid and glue it. Tie another length into a small bow and glue the bow over the seam.

2

Turn the lid upside down and squeeze waterproof glue into the inside of the lid. Press the base of the ornament into the glue (right) and allow it to dry overnight.

3

Pour distilled water into the jar, filling it to the base of the neck. Leave about ¾ inch of air space so that the water will be able to rise without overflowing when the lid and ornament are screwed into place.

4

Sprinkle approximately a tablespoon of nonmetallic white glitter into the jar, so the glitter covers the bottom generously.

5

Squeeze the glue along the inner edge of the lid to create a seal when it is tightened. Screw the lid to the jar. Once the glue is thoroughly dry, turn the jar over, shake it, and watch the snow fall.

Spinning Valentine

Ages 4 to 6

When you spin this, the heart and lips, on opposite sides, will form one image.

Materials

jar lid, 2½ inches across
pencil
white posterboard or cardboard
red construction paper
glue
red lipstick
lollipop stick or pencil
transparent tape
safety scissors

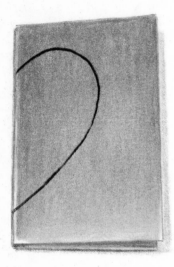

1

Outline the lid on the posterboard and cut out the circle. Fold the red paper down the middle and draw half a heart on the fold (above). Cut it out and glue it to the circle (above, right). Put lipstick on and kiss the other side of the circle (right).

2

Tape the circle to the end of a lollipop stick or pencil (right). To spin the valentine, hold the stick between your palms and rub your hands rapidly back and forth (top).

A Circle of Hearts

Ages 4 to 6

You can mount this valentine on a sheet of white paper or a paper doily.

Materials

pot lid
lightweight red paper
pencil
safety scissors

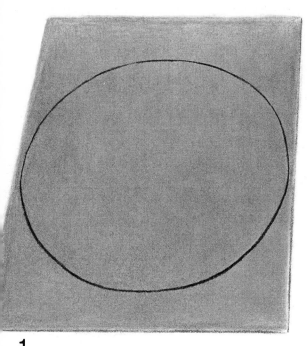

1

Place the lid on a sheet of the paper, trace around it, and cut out the circle. Fold the circle in half.

2

Fold the half-circle in half (above); then fold the quarter-circle in half, forming an eighth. Draw a heart on the face of the eighth, wide enough so the sides form hinges (right). Cut out the heart, avoiding the hinges. Unfold.

Pop-Up Valentine

Ages 4 to 6

You can send this valentine just as it is or mount it on the front of a folded construction-paper card.

Materials

red and white construction paper
pencil
safety scissors
glue

1

Fold a sheet of red construction paper in half. Draw half a heart, using the fold line as a center line; trim it. Draw a second, smaller heart on white construction paper, and cut it out as well.

2

For the spring, cut one red strip and a matching white strip from the construction paper, each about ½ to ¾ inch wide and 4 to 6 inches long. Glue one end of the two strips together into an L shape (below).

3

*To make the spring, fold
the bottom strip over the
intersection (below). Then
fold the other strip over
the intersection. Continue
folding in this way until
the two strips are used up.*

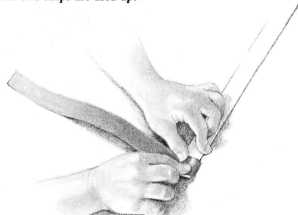

4

*To finish the valentine,
glue one end of the spring
to the center of the larger
heart (below). Then
glue the other end to the
center of the smaller heart.*

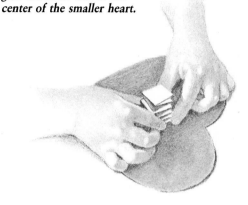

Love Collage

Ages 3 to 6

A collage, using variations on heart
shapes, makes a wonderful valentine.

*Cut several hearts at once by folding a sheet
of colored construction paper into thirds or quarters.
Glue the hearts, as well as the sheets from which
they were cut, on background paper.*

Shamrock Napkin Rings

Ages 4 to 6

You can adapt this St. Patrick's Day project to any holiday simply by changing the felt decoration.

Materials

3-by-5-inch file cards
pen
green felt
safety scissors
glue
stapler

1

On a file card, draw a shamrock about 2½ inches across; cut it out to make a pattern. Outline the pattern on a piece of felt, once for each napkin ring you intend to make (above). Cut out the felt shamrocks.

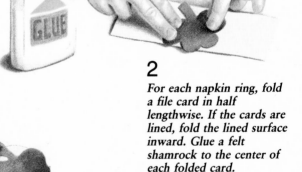

2

For each napkin ring, fold a file card in half lengthwise. If the cards are lined, fold the lined surface inward. Glue a felt shamrock to the center of each folded card.

3

When the glue has dried, roll the card into a ring, shamrock side out, overlapping the ends about ½ inch, and staple the overlapped ends together, top and bottom.

Easter-Egg Collages

Ages 4 to 6

This egg-decorating technique does not
require any egg dye or food coloring.

*Gather a selection of ribbons, stickers, stars, and
scraps of colorful fabric and paper. With a pair of
scissors, a container of glue, and a supply of
hard-boiled eggs, you can create highly personal
collages. Parents can provide help with such
finishing touches as bows.*

Polka-Dot Eggs

Ages 4 to 6

For egg decorating, cotton swabs give
more control than brushes.

*Prepare commercial Easter-egg dye according to
package directions or use food coloring diluted
in cups. Provide a cotton swab for each color. Make
the polka dots by pressing the tip of a color-dipped
swab against the egg and stroke on color by using the
cotton swab as a brush.*

Crayon Eggs

Ages 4 to 6

The crayon resists dye, revealing a
pattern when the egg is colored.

*Write or draw on a hard-boiled egg with an ordinary
white crayon. When the decoration is complete, lower
the egg with tongs into a disposable cup half-filled
with commercial Easter-egg dye or with water mixed
with food coloring; leave the egg in the dye long
enough to get a strong contrast between the crayoned
and noncrayoned areas—one to three minutes.*

Two-Tone Eggs

Ages 4 to 6

This egg-decorating technique uses
masking tape to resist the dye.

*Tint hard-boiled eggs by immersing them briefly in
commercial Easter-egg dye or in food coloring mixed
with water. Dry the eggs with paper towels. Decorate
the eggs with bits of masking tape cut into stripes,
squares, and random shapes. When the design is
complete, reimmerse the egg in the dye, leaving it
there until the shell's color is intense. Remove the egg,
allow it to dry, and then carefully pull off the tape.
Some of the dye will have seeped beneath the tape,
making the egg appear to be tie-dyed.*

Marbled Eggs

Ages 4 to 6

Adult participation required

Materials

hard-boiled eggs
piece of cotton cloth, about 6 inches
    square
rubber bands
commercial Easter-egg dye or food
    coloring
disposable plastic cups for dye
medicine dropper

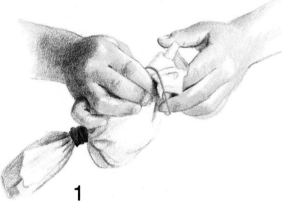

1

To prepare each egg for dyeing, dampen the piece of cotton cloth and wrap it around the egg. Secure the cloth at each end of the egg with a rubber band.

2

Prepare commercial Easter-egg dye in several colors or add drops of food coloring to half-filled cups of water. Use a medicine dropper to dribble one color at random over the cloth-covered egg. Rinse the medicine dropper and apply more colors.

3

When you have applied several colors, twist the ends of the cloth, forcing the colors to run together. Wait several minutes, then unwrap the egg and allow it to dry. Rinse out the cloth, wring it out, and use it to wrap a second egg.

Hand-Print Tulip

Ages 4 to 5

Materials
two plastic-foam meat trays
red and green tempera paint
construction or typing paper

1
Place the trays on either
side of the paper and pour
a tablespoon of paint into
each of them. To make the
flower, dip the palm of
one hand in the red paint
and press your palm
against the paper, near
the top edge.

2
To make the stem, dip the
little finger and side of
your other hand in the
green paint and press them
on the paper, just below
the flower. For a longer
stem, recoat your little
finger and place it beneath
your first print.

3
To make leaves, use the
hand with which you made
the stem. Dip the outside
in the green paint,
including the heel of your
hand. Press down on
the paper at an angle to
the stem, on each side.

Bunny Bag

Ages 3 to 4

Your children can use this bag
to collect hidden Easter eggs they
have decorated for each other
(pages 113-115).

Materials

white sandwich or bakery bag
water-based felt-tip markers or crayons
safety scissors
yarn and stickers
glue
construction paper
stapler (optional)

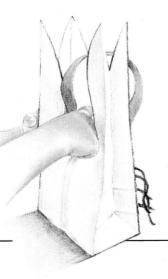

1

*Using the picture above as
a guide, draw ears along
the sides of the flattened
bag. Cut along the drawn
line, through both the
front and back.*

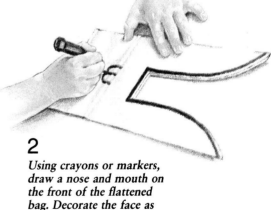

2

*Using crayons or markers,
draw a nose and mouth on
the front of the flattened
bag. Decorate the face as
you choose, adding stickers
for eyes and attaching
yarn whiskers with glue.*

3

*For the handle, cut a strip
of construction paper
1 inch wide and 9 inches
long. Open the bag and
glue or staple the strip to
the inside front and
back of the bag, between
the bunny's ears.*

117

Matzo Cover

Ages 4 to 6

Adult participation required

This cover holds the three pieces of matzo traditionally placed on the Seder table during Passover meals.

Materials

four 7-inch squares of tissue paper
  (two of blue, two of white)
hole punch
36-inch length of white or blue yarn
masking tape
glue

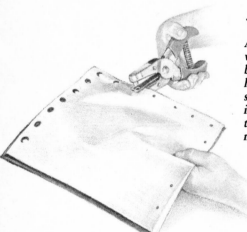

1

Align the squares of paper, with the blue sheets between the white. Punch holes for stitching three sides, 1 inch apart and ¼ inch from the edge. Save the punched circles for the matzo cover's decoration.

3

Decorate the matzo cover with the circles punched from the lacing holes, gluing them in a design. A parent can write the word "matzo" on the front of the completed cover.

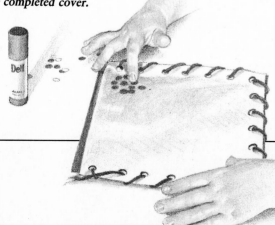

2

Knot one end of the yarn, and wrap the other with tape for easy lacing. Poke the yarn through the first hole, pulling it to the knot. Bring it over the edge and through the second hole. Repeat until you have laced three sides. Clip off the tape; knot.

Foil Elijah Cup

Ages 4 to 6

This is a variation on the goblet traditionally filled with wine for the prophet Elijah at the Passover Seder.

Materials

small piece of corrugated cardboard
plastic-foam drinking cup
pencil
safety scissors
small plastic cup
empty thread spool, large size
glue
18-inch length of aluminum foil

1

To make the goblet base, trace the top of the plastic-foam cup on the piece of cardboard; cut out. Form the stem of the goblet by gluing one end of the spool to the center of the cardboard disk.

2

Apply glue generously to the bottom of the plastic-foam cup, and press the cup firmly against the top of the spool. Allow the glue to dry thoroughly.

3

Place the goblet on the foil, and wrap the foil around the base. Continue wrapping, pressing the foil around the stem and cup. Lap the foil over the lip. Insert the clear cup.

Cotton-Ball Popper

Ages 3 to 6
Adult participation required

Materials
tube from a roll of paper towels
tube from a gift-wrap or other roll
 narrow enough to fit inside the
 paper-towel tube
serrated knife or coping saw
crayons or water-based felt-tip markers
nonmetallic glitter
glue
cotton balls

1

Measure the length of the paper-towel tube and mark the narrower gift-wrap tube to a length an inch or two longer. Cut the narrower tube to length using a serrated knife or a coping saw.

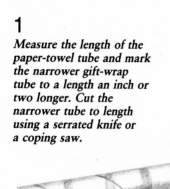

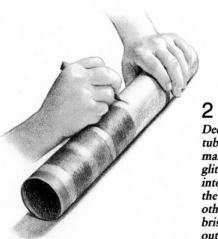

2

Decorate the paper-towel tube with crayons or markers and glued-on glitter. Pack cotton balls into one end of it. Insert the narrow tube into the other end, and push it briskly forward to force out the cotton balls.

Your Own Flag

Ages 4 to 6
Adult participation required

Look at flags in an encyclopedia, then have your child design his own flag.

Materials
colored construction paper
safety scissors
glue
nonmetallic glitter
½-inch dowel or stick for flagstaff
masking tape

1

Cut stripes, stars, and other shapes from the paper. Glue them to a background sheet. Dribble glue over the flag and shake glitter on top. Stand the flag on edge and tap it gently to release excess glitter. Let the glue dry.

2

Turn the flag over and place the dowel an inch or so from the edge where you want the flagstaff to be, aligning the dowel with the edge. Tape the dowel to the flag.

Circle Pumpkin

Ages 5 to 6
Adult participation required

You can turn this Halloween pumpkin into a Christmas ornament by substituting red paper for orange.

Materials
orange and green construction paper
jar lid or saucer
pencil
safety scissors
glue

1

Holding the lid or saucer firmly in place on a sheet of orange construction paper, outline it ten times to make ten circles.

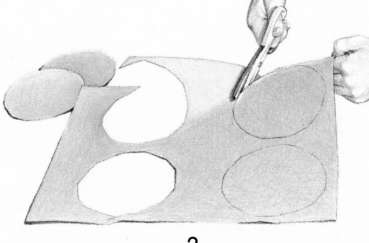

2

Use safety scissors to cut out the circles, being careful to follow the pencil lines as closely as possible so that all the circles will be the same size.

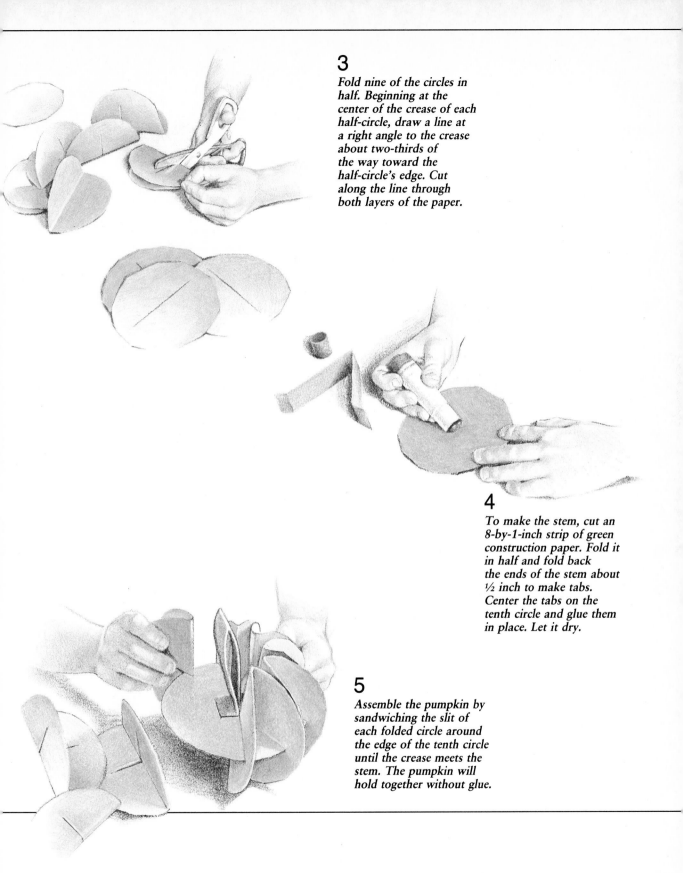

3

Fold nine of the circles in half. Beginning at the center of the crease of each half-circle, draw a line at a right angle to the crease about two-thirds of the way toward the half-circle's edge. Cut along the line through both layers of the paper.

4

To make the stem, cut an 8-by-1-inch strip of green construction paper. Fold it in half and fold back the ends of the stem about ½ inch to make tabs. Center the tabs on the tenth circle and glue them in place. Let it dry.

5

Assemble the pumpkin by sandwiching the slit of each folded circle around the edge of the tenth circle until the crease meets the stem. The pumpkin will hold together without glue.

Spider on a Web

Ages 5 to 6

Adult participation required

Materials

black and orange construction paper
mixing bowl
pen
heavy-duty scissors
stapler
glue
length of string
one-half package of white crepe paper

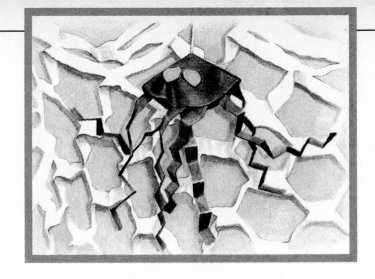

1

Place a mixing bowl upside down on a sheet of black construction paper. With a pen, outline the rim to form a circle for the body (left). Cut it out.

2

Locate the center of the circle by folding it in half, then in quarters. Unfold and make a cut along one crease from the edge to the center (left).

3

Shape the circle into a shallow cone by slightly overlapping the cut sides. Staple the sides together.

4

Cut a sheet of black construction paper into eight 1-inch-wide strips for legs. Fold each leg accordion-style (below).

5

Glue the legs to the bottom of the body. Cut eyes out of the orange construction paper and glue them in place. Make a small hole in the peak of the body and thread a string, knotted at one end, through it for hanging.

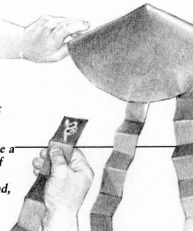

6

For the web, cut a package
of white crepe paper in
half crosswise. Using only
one half, turn down the
free top flap. Working
from each edge of the top
folded sheet, draw lines
1 inch apart and to within
1 inch of the edge opposite
the one they were drawn
from (above).

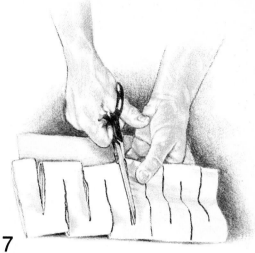

7

Cut along the lines with
scissors, making sure
to cut through the entire
thickness of the paper.

8

Holding the top flap,
gently shake the strips of
crepe paper loose (right).
To achieve a weblike look,
hang the crepe paper
from one of its long sides
with the spider on it.

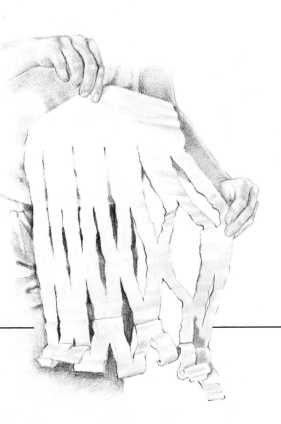

Scarecrow Mobile

Ages 5 to 6
Adult participation required

If you loop the end of the string through a hook in the ceiling, this mobile will dance in air currents.

Materials
pencil
construction paper in several colors
safety scissors
crayons or water-based markers
glue
string or yarn

1

Using the illustration below as a guide, draw outlines for (clockwise from top right) a shirt, a hat, pants, and a pumpkin head on pieces of folded construction paper.

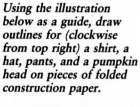

2

Cut out the parts, then use them as patterns to cut duplicates for each, providing a front and a back for the scarecrow. Make sure they match well. Decorate one side of all eight pieces in any way you like.

3

Lay in a vertical row, right sides down, one hat, head, shirt, and pants, leaving space between them. Apply glue along the center of the pieces and press a length of string or yarn on it. Add more glue; press the other parts, face up, against their mates.

A Party to Set Spirits Soaring

Few occasions offer more opportunity for just plain fun than Halloween, and a costume party planned around the event is bound to please four- to six-year-olds. The following pages offer suggestions calculated to make a party for your youngster and his friends a success. If you are leery about their enthusiasm getting out of hand, limit the number of guests and make sure that you have adult or teenage helpers on hand for the occasion.

When planning the party, keep in mind that some youngsters are easily frightened. Darkened rooms and spooky music may scare them. And while the children will revel in one another's costumes, they will probably be more comfortable if the adults present are dressed in their regular everyday clothes rather than in disguise.

Plan your party for afternoon, perhaps around three o'clock, and offer an assortment of healthful finger foods—cut-up fruit, bits of cheese, bite-size peanut-butter sandwiches. If you end the party with a trick-or-treat walk around the neighborhood, the foods will have done much to keep energies from flagging and forestall indiscriminate consumption of candies bestowed.

Cheerful pumpkins, floppy bats, and a friendly ghost welcome a ballerina and her mother to a daytime Halloween celebration. Decorations have been kept simple. The construction-paper bats are taped to the corner pillar, and the bed-sheet ghost, whose head is a round pillow tied inside the center of the sheet, is suspended by strings from the porch ceiling.

The ballerina and skeleton admire a ghost's pumpkin artistry as a witch works intently on her own design. Have a pumpkin for each child you invite, as well as a supply of markers and crayons so that the guests will be able to personalize pumpkins to take home with them. Choose smooth-skinned pumpkins small enough for youngsters to handle but large enough for them to decorate.

Quaking in mock fear, the ghost is surprised by a mysterious stranger, but the unfazed superhero concentrates on decorating a trick-or-treat bag. Have a supply of small shopping bags with handles available for youngsters to embellish. And have plain masks ready for decorating: Cut eyeholes from paper plates, and tape a tongue depressor to the back of each one to serve as a handle. Supply the children with cotton balls, stickers, scraps, glue, and markers with which to liven up the masks.

Helped along by an open-mouthed audience, the ballerina stands en pointe as she reaches for her tasty prize. For this simple variation on bobbing for apples, suspend doughnuts from ribbons attached to a doorframe. As each child succeeds in biting a doughnut without using helping hands, remove it so that she can enjoy the remainder as her prize.

The witch and ballerina decorate the straw-filled, paper-bag head of a pint-size scarecrow while the other children stuff pants and shirts. Knot the cuffs and ankles of cast-off or thrift-shop children's clothing and let each youngster create an individualized scarecrow. (Leaves or rags may be substituted for straw.) Attach the stuffed garments together with large safety pins. Insert each head into the collar of a shirt, and tie the collar securely with string.

A happy pandemonium reigns as the children explore a cardboard-box tunnel and an appliance-box haunted house. To make similar props, join the flaps of boxes for the tunnel with heavy-duty tape. Cut out a doorway from the appliance box and hang black crepe-paper streamers across the entrance. You can ensure just the right Halloween touch by adding a paper spider and web (pages 124-125), a pumpkin, and construction-paper bats. Count on the partygoers' vivid imaginations and spontaneous sound effects to complete the scene.

Armed with personal trick-or-treat bags and jack-o'-lantern flashlights, the guests go on a round of neighbors' homes. For the lights, use panels from brown-paper lunch bags, snip out features, and wrap the faces over the head of each flashlight. Cover these with orange tissue paper and tie both tightly with yarn. Trim any excess paper. Since the flashlights will emit only an orange glow, accompany the children with an unadorned flashlight of your own.

Turkey Decoration

Ages 4 to 6
Adult participation required

This turkey makes a charming centerpiece for the Thanksgiving dinner table.

Materials
brown-paper lunch bag
newspapers
yarn or string
colored construction paper
safety scissors
glue
water-based felt-tip markers

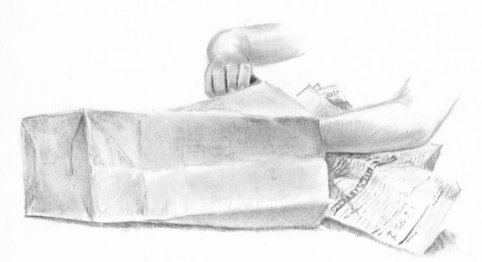

1
To make the turkey's body, crumple two double sheets of newspaper and stuff them inside the brown-paper lunch bag. Push the newspaper firmly into the bag so that it fills the corners completely.

2
Cut a 10-inch piece of yarn or string and tie it in a secure knot around the bag opening, an inch or two from the end. Fan open the end of the bag to make a base for the tail feathers (right).

3

Cut out eight or more tail feathers from construction paper of various colors and fringe the edges of the feathers with the scissors. Glue the feathers to the fanned-out end of the paper bag (below).

4

For the head, fold a sheet of construction paper in half. Using the illustration below as a guide, outline the head, with the beak at the crease. After cutting, bend back the edges of the neck for tabs. From a separate sheet of paper, cut out the turkey's two feet.

5

Apply glue to the tabs on the turkey's neck and press them against the bottom of the bag. Turn the turkey upside down and glue the two feet in place. Use markers to draw eyes and feathers on the decoration.

Star of David

Ages 4 to 6
Adult participation required

Materials
white pipe cleaners
blue yarn
safety scissors

1

Make a triangle from three pipe cleaners by bending their ends into hooks and linking them. Twist the ends together. Make a second triangle.

2

Place one triangle on top of the other to form a six-pointed star. Tie a piece of yarn around each of the joints where the two triangles meet.

3

To finish the star, cut an 8-inch length of yarn and loop it through one of the points of the star. Knot the ends of the yarn together, forming a hanger.

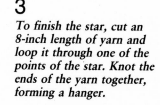

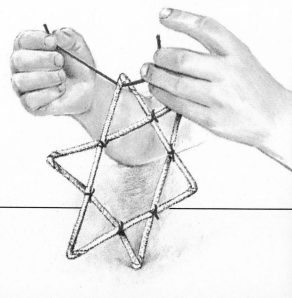

Clay Menorah

Ages 4 to 6
Adult participation required

Materials
self-hardening clay
Hanukkah candles
tempera paint
paintbrush

1

To form the base of
the menorah, roll self-
hardening clay into a
1-inch-thick rope about 24
inches long (above). Form
the rope into a circle,
joining the ends together
firmly (right).

2

Roll additional clay into a
1-inch ball; make nine
more. Press a Hanukkah
candle into each of nine
balls and rotate the candle
to widen the opening.
The opening will shrink as
the clay dries.

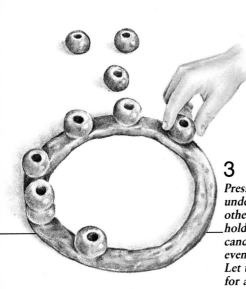

3

Press the tenth ball
underneath one of the
others to form the tall
holder for the shammash
candle. Press the balls
evenly around the circle.
Let the menorah dry
for a day or longer before
you paint it.

Tree and Wreath

Ages 4 to 6
Adult participation required

Materials
12-inch posterboard square
paper plate
pencil
safety scissors
masking tape
stapler
green and red tissue paper
glue
unbreakable bowl

1

To form the tree, draw an arc from one corner of the posterboard to the corner diagonally opposite. Cut along the arc.

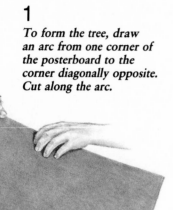

2

Roll the posterboard into a cone, with the straight edges overlapping. Have someone hold the cone in shape while you tape the straight edges together.

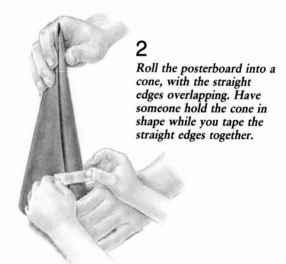

To make a wreath. *Cut around a paper plate's rim and remove the center. Tape the rim together and decorate with paper bits.*

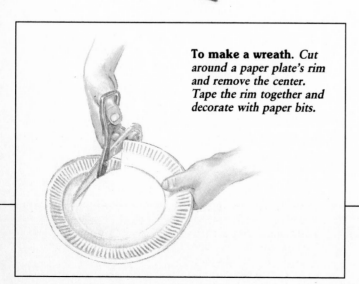

3

Tear and crumple 2-inch pieces of tissue. Pour some glue into a bowl. Dip the pieces of the crumpled tissue into the glue and press them onto the cone.

Dough Ornaments

Ages 4 to 6

Adult participation required

Materials

salt dough or cornstarch dough *(recipes, page 80)*
wax paper
rolling pin
cookie cutters
pencil
plastic knife
watercolor paints and brush
shellac
yarn or metallic cord

1

Roll out the dough on wax paper to a thickness no less than ¼ inch so that the ornaments will not be too fragile. Cut out with cookie cutters.

2

Draw designs in the dough shapes with a pencil or a plastic knife and add details with bits of dough. Use the point of a pencil to poke a hole through each ornament for a hanger. Then let the ornaments dry overnight.

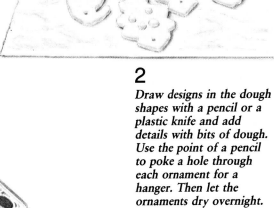

3

When the ornaments are dry, decorate them with watercolors, then shellac them. Loop yarn through the holes in the ornaments to serve as hangers.

Index-Card Ornaments

Ages 5 to 6

Adult participation required

These basic techniques can be used to create a variety of Christmas ornaments.

Materials

unlined 3-by-5-inch index cards
glue
safety scissors
hole punch
decorative cord or yarn

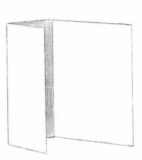

1

Fold an index card in half crosswise and crease the fold line (far left). Fold each edge to meet the crease (center left), creating an open, four-sided shape (near left). Repeat this process three times.

2

Glue the four shapes together along their middle surfaces (left). Allow the glue to dry before proceeding any further.

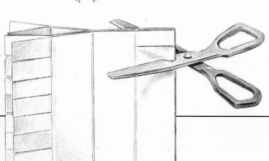

3

Flatten the assembled cards and fringe the open sides, cutting through all four layers (far left). Punch a hole for a hanger near the top of the center crease, and press the ornament back into shape. Thread cord or yarn through the hole to form a hanger.

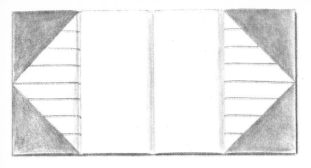

For a fringed diamond design, assemble cards as in Steps 1 and 2. Flatten the cards and cut the open edges into triangles (far left). Fringe them to the nearest crease, and press back into shape (near left).

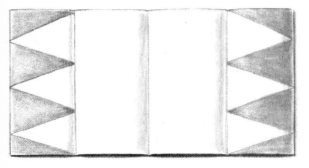

For a zigzag design, assemble cards as in Steps 1 and 2. Flatten them and cut out a zigzag pattern (far left). Then make the points meet for a prism effect (near left).

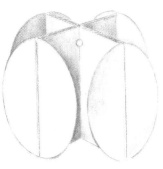

By curving the open edges of the flattened cards (far left), you will create an ornament with four oval panels (near left) on which you can paint or paste Christmas designs.

Bibliography

BOOKS

Ames, Louise Bates, *The Gesell Institute's Child from One to Six: Evaluating the Behavior of the Preschool Child.* New York: Harper & Row, 1979.

Becker, Joyce, *Hanukkah Crafts.* New York: Bonim Books, 1978.

Bland, Jane Cooper, *Art of the Young Child.* New York: Museum of Modern Art, 1957.

Boston Children's Medical Center and Elizabeth M. Gregg, *What to Do When "There's Nothing to Do."* New York: Dell Publishing Co., 1968.

Braga, Laurie, and Joseph Braga, *Learning and Growing: A Guide to Child Development.* Englewood Cliffs, N.J.: Prentice-Hall, 1975.

Breckenridge, Marian E., and E. Lee Vincent, *Child Development: Physical and Psychological Growth through Adolescence.* Philadelphia: W. B. Saunders Co., 1965.

Brinn, Ruth Esrig, *Let's Celebrate!* Silver Spring, Md.: Kar-Ben Copies, 1977.

Brittain, W. Lambert, *Creativity, Art, and the Young Child.* New York: Macmillan Publishing Co., 1979.

Caney, Steven, *Kids' America.* New York: Workman Publishing Co., 1978.

Caplan, Theresa, and Frank Caplan, *The Early Childhood Years: The 2- to 6-Year-Old.* New York: Bantam Books, 1983.

Chernoff, Goldie Taub, *Clay-Dough Play-Dough.* New York: Walker and Company, 1974.

Cherry, Clare, *Creative Art for the Developing Child: A Teacher's Handbook for Early Childhood Education.* Belmont, Calif.: Fearon-Pitman Publishers, 1972.

Choate, Judith, and Jane Green, *Scrapcraft: 50 Easy-To-Make Handicraft Projects.* Garden City, N.Y.: Doubleday & Company, 1973.

Cohen, Elaine Pear, and Ruth Straus Gainer, *Art: Another Language for Learning.* New York: Schocken Books, 1984.

Cohen, Marilyn A., and Pamela J. Gross, *The Developmental Resource: Behavioral Sequences for Assessment and Program Planning.* 2 vols. New York: Grune & Stratton, 1979.

Cole, Ann, et al., *A Pumpkin in a Pear Tree: Creative Ideas for Twelve Months of Holiday Fun.* Boston: Little, Brown and Co., 1976.

Cole, Ann, Carolyn Haas, and Betty Weinberger, *Purple Cow to the Rescue.* Boston: Little, Brown and Co., 1982.

Cooper, Stephanie, Christine Fynes-Clinton, and Marye Rowling, *The Children's Year: Crafts and Clothes for Children and Parents to Make.* Whiteshill, Gloucester, England: Hawthorn Press, 1986.

Coskey, Evelyn, *Easter Eggs for Everyone.* Nashville: Abingdon Press, 1973.

Einon, Dorothy, *Play with a Purpose: Learning Games for Children Six Weeks to Ten Years.* New York: Pantheon Books, 1985.

The Family Creative Workshop. Vol. 11. New York: Plenary Publications International, 1975.

Fiarotta, Phyllis, and Noel Fiarotta, *Be What You Want to Be!* New York: Workman Publishing Co., 1977.

Gardner, Howard, *Frames of Mind: The Theory of Multiple Intelligences.* New York: Basic Books, 1983.

Haas, Carolyn, Ann Cole, and Barbara Naftzger, *Backyard Vacation: Outdoor Fun in Your Own Neighborhood.* Boston: Little, Brown and Co., 1980.

Holz, Loretta, *Mobiles You Can Make.* New York: Lothrop, Lee & Shepard Co., 1975.

Jenkins, Peggy Davison, *Art for the Fun of It: A Guide for Teaching Young Children.* Englewood Cliffs, N.J.: Prentice-Hall, 1980.

Kohl, Mary Ann F., *Scribble Cookies.* Bellingham, Wash.: Bright Ring Publishing, 1985.

Lasky, Lila, and Rose Mukerji, *Art: Basic for Young Children.* Washington, D.C.: The National Association for the Education of Young Children, 1984.

Lewis, Hilda Present, ed., *Child Art: The Beginnings of Self-Assertion.* Berkeley, Calif.: Diablo Press, 1973.

Lowenfeld, Viktor, and W. Lambert Brittain, *Creative and Mental Growth.* New York: Macmillan Publishing Co., 1982.

Mayesky, Mary, *Creative Activities for Young Children.* Albany, N.Y.: Delmar Publishers, 1985.

Mell, Howard, and Eric Fisher, *Working with Paper.* New York: Drake Publishers, 1971.

The Merriment of Christmas, by the Editors of *Life.* Vol. 3 of *The Life Book of Christmas.* New York: Time Inc., 1963.

Mussen, Paul H., *The Psychological Development of the Child.* Englewood Cliffs, N.J.: Prentice-Hall, 1963.

Newsome, Arden J., *Egg Craft.* New York: Lothrop, Lee & Shepard Co., 1973.

Parish, Peggy, *December Decorations: A Holiday How-to Book.* New York: Macmillan Publishing Co., 1975.

Perry, Margaret, *Rainy Day Magic: The Art of Making Sunshine on a Stormy Day.* New York: M. Evans and Co., 1970.

Pitcher, Evelyn G., Sylvia G. Feinburg, and David Alexander, *Helping Young Children Learn.* Columbus, Ohio: Charles E. Merrill Publishing Co., 1984.

Purdy, Susan, *Festivals for You to Celebrate.* Philadelphia: J. B. Lippincott Co., 1969.

Robbins, Ireene, *Arts and Crafts Media Ideas for the Elementary Teacher.* West Nyack, N.Y.: Parker Publishing Co., 1973.

Robinson, Jeri, *Activities for Anyone, Anytime, Anywhere.* Boston: Little, Brown and Co., 1983.

Rockwell, Harlow, *Printmaking.* Garden City, N.Y.: Doubleday & Co., 1973.

Rosen, Clare, *Making Presents.* London: Usborne Publishing, 1984.

Sanford, Anne R., and Janet G. Zelman, *LAP: The Learning Accomplishment Profile.* Winston-Salem, N.C.: Kaplan Press, 1981.

Schickedanz, Judith A., et. al., *Strategies for Teaching Young Children.* Englewood Cliffs, N.J.: Prentice-Hall, 1983.

Schickedanz, Judith A., David I. Schickedanz, and Peggy D. Forsyth, *Toward Understanding Children.* Boston: Little, Brown and Co., 1982.

Seidelman, James E., and Grace Mintonye, *Shopping Cart Art.* New York: The Macmillan Co., 1970.

Sharon, Ruth, *Arts and Crafts the Year Round.* Vol. 1. New York: United Synagogue Commission on Jewish Education, 1972.

Silberstein-Storfer, Muriel, and Mablen Jones, *Doing Art Together.* New York: Simon and Schuster, 1982.

Simons, Robin, *Recyclopedia: Games, Science Equipment, and Crafts from Recycled Materials.* Boston: Houghton Mifflin Co., 1976.

Sommer, Elyse, *The Bread Dough Craft Book.* New York: Lothrop, Lee & Shepard Co., 1972.

Spizman, Robyn Freedman, *Lollipop Grapes and Clothespin Critters.* Reading, Mass.: Addison-Wesley Publishing Co., 1985.

Stein, Sara Bonnett, *The Kids' Kitchen Takeover.* New York: Workman Publishing Co., 1975.

Stewart, Linda Martin, ed., *Christmas Is Coming! 1987.* Birmingham Ala.: Oxmoor House, 1987.

Striker, Susan, *Please Touch: How to Stimulate Your Child's Creative Development.* New York: Simon & Schuster, 1986.

Temko, Florence, *Paper Cutting.* Garden City, N.Y.: Doubleday & Co., 1973.

White, Burton L., *The First Three Years of Life.* Englewood Cliffs, N.J.: Prentice-Hall, 1975.

Wilson, Sue, *I Can Do It! I Can Do It! Arts & Crafts for the Mentally Retarded.* New York: Quail Street Publishing Co., 1976.

Wood, Annette, *Teaching Art & Crafts in Elementary School.* Englewood Cliffs, N.J.: Prentice-Hall, 1981.

PERIODICAL

Simmons, Thomas, "Why Kids Love Making Art." *Parenting,* August 1987.

Acknowledgments and Picture Credits

The index for this book was prepared by Louise Hedberg. The editors also thank: Roslyn Beitler, Washington, D.C.; Joanne Gigliotti, Washington, D.C.; Betty MacDonald, McLean, Va.; Sherry Olstein, Falls Church, Va.; Pat Peat O'Neil, Silver Spring, Md.; Marjorie Pitts, Washington, D.C.

All photographs were taken by Roger Foley.

The sources for the illustrations in this book are listed below. Credits from left to right are separated by semicolons; credits from top to bottom are separated by dashes.

Illustrations. 7-17: Donald Gates from photos by Beecie Kupersmith. 21: Donald Gates from photos by Marilyn Segall. 22: Donald Gates from photos by Jane Jordan, except child's rendering at lower left. 23: Child's rendering—Donald Gates from photo by Jane Jordan. 24, 25: William Hennessy, Jr., from photos by Marilyn Segall. 26: William Hennessy, Jr., from photos by Jane Jordan. 27: William Hennessy, Jr., from photos by Jane Jordan. Project conceptualized by Michael Small. 28: Elizabeth Wolf from photos by Marilyn Segall. 29-31: Elizabeth Wolf from photos by Marilyn Segall. Project conceptualized by Linda Blaser. 33: Diagram by Tina Taylor. Art by Elizabeth Wolf from photo by Marilyn Segall. 34: Elizabeth Wolf from photo by Jane Jordan. 35: Child's rendering. 36: Donald Gates from photos by Marilyn Segall. 37: Child's rendering copied by Larry Sherer—Donald Gates from photos by Marilyn Segall (2). 38: Donald Gates from photos by Beecie Kupersmith, except child's rendering at upper right. 39: Donald Gates from photos by Beecie Kupersmith. 40: Donald Gates from photo by Marilyn Segall—child's renderings (2). 41: Child's renderings (2)—Donald Gates from photos by Beecie Kupersmith (2). 42: Child's rendering—Donald Gates from photos by Beecie Kupersmith (2). 43: Donald Gates from photos by Beecie Kupersmith. 44: Child's rendering—Donald Gates from photos by Beecie Kupersmith (3). 45: Donald Gates from photos by Beecie Kupersmith. 46: Lisa F. Semerad from photo by Beecie Kupersmith. 47-49: Lisa F. Semerad from photos by Beecie Kupersmith. Project conceptualized by Carol Boyd. 50-54: Diagram by Tina Taylor. Art by Elizabeth Wolf, from photos by Beecie Kupersmith. Project conceptualized by Beecie Kupersmith. 55: William Hennessy, Jr., from photos by Beecie Kupersmith. 56, 57: William Hennessy, Jr., from photos by Beecie Kupersmith. Project conceptualized by Vial Crouch. 58, 59: Lisa F. Semerad from photos by Jane Jordan. 60: Lisa F. Semerad from photos by Beecie Kupersmith. Project conceptualized by Alice Cannon. 61-63: Lisa F. Semerad from photos by Jane Jordan. Project conceptualized by Alice Cannon. 64, 65: Elizabeth Wolf from photos by Beecie Kupersmith. Project conceptualized by Beecie Kupersmith. 66-69: Elizabeth Wolf from photos by Beecie Kupersmith. Project conceptualized by Carol Boyd. 70-75: Diagram by Tina Taylor. Art by Marguerite E. Bell from photos by Beecie Kupersmith. Project conceptualized by Beecie Kupersmith. 76: Donald Gates from photos by Marilyn Segall. Projects conceptualized by Ann Miller. 77: Donald Gates from photos by Jane Jordan. Project conceptualized by Dorothy Wallace. 78, 79: Donald Gates from photos by Beecie Kupersmith. 81-83: Donald Gates from photos by Marilyn Segall. 84, 85: William Hennessy, Jr., from photos by Beecie Kupersmith. Project conceptualized by Holly Langenfeld. 86-89: William Hennessy, Jr., from photos by Beecie Kupersmith. 90, 91: Marguerite E. Bell from photos by Marilyn Segall. 92, 93: Marguerite E. Bell from photos by Jane Jordan. 94, 95: Elizabeth Wolf. 96, 97: Elizabeth Wolf from photos by Marilyn Segall. 100: Lisa F. Semerad from photo by Marilyn Segall—from photos by Jane Jordan (2). 101: Lisa F. Semerad from photos by Jane Jordan. 102, 103: Lisa F. Semerad from photos by Beecie Kupersmith. 104: Marguerite E. Bell from photos by Jane Jordan. 105: Marguerite E. Bell from photos by Jane Jordan. Project conceptualized by Alice Cannon. 106, 107: William Hennessy, Jr., from photos by Jane Jordan. 108, 109: William Hennessy, Jr., from photos by Jane Jordan. Projects conceptualized by Lorene Steinberg. 110, 111: Pop-up valentine art by Marguerite E. Bell from photos by Beecie Kupersmith. Project conceptualized by Lorene Steinberg. Cutout valentine art by Marguerite E. Bell from photo by Jane Jordan; child's rendering copied by Larry Sherer. 112: Lisa F. Semerad from photos by Marilyn Segall. Project conceptualized by Nancy Payne. 113-115: Lisa F. Semerad from photos by Beecie Kupersmith. 116: Marguerite E. Bell from photos by Jane Jordan, except child's rendering at top. 117: Marguerite E. Bell from photos by Jane Jordan. 118, 119: Marguerite E. Bell from photos by Marilyn Segall. 120: Lisa F. Semerad from photos by Jane Jordan. 121: Lisa F. Semerad from photos by Marilyn Segall. 122, 123: Marguerite E. Bell from photos by Marilyn Segall. 124-131: Marguerite E. Bell from photos by Beecie Kupersmith. 132, 133: William Hennessy, Jr., from photos by Beecie Kupersmith. 134-136: William Hennessy, Jr., from photos by Marilyn Segall. 137: William Hennessy, Jr., from photos by Beecie Kupersmith. 138: William Hennessy, Jr., from photo by Beecie Kupersmith—William Hennessy, Jr. (4). 139: William Hennessy, Jr.

Index